双双中文教材（18）
Chinese Language and Culture Course

中国古代哲学 Ancient Chinese Philosophy

王双双 编著

北京大学出版社
PEKING UNIVERSITY PRESS

图书在版编目（CIP）数据

中国古代哲学/王双双 编著.—北京：北京大学出版社，2007.7
（双双中文教材18）
ISBN 978-7-301-08709-1

Ⅰ.中…　Ⅱ.王…　Ⅲ.汉语-对外汉语教学-教材　Ⅳ.H195.4

中国版本图书馆CIP数据核字（2005）第075451号

书　　　　名：	中国古代哲学
著作责任者：	王双双　编著
英文翻译：	陶友兰
责任编辑：	孙　娴　suzannex@126.com
标准书号：	ISBN 978-7-301-08709-1/H·1445
出版发行：	北京大学出版社
地　　　　址：	北京市海淀区成府路205号　100871
网　　　　址：	http://www.pup.cn
电　　　　话：	邮购部 62752015　发行部 62750672　编辑部 62752028　出版部 62754962
电子信箱：	zpup@pup.pku.edu.cn
印刷者：	北京大学印刷厂
经销者：	新华书店

　　　　　　889毫米×1194毫米　16开本　8.5印张　119千字
　　　　　　2007年7月第1版　2018年9月第5次印刷

定　　　　价：76.00元（含课本、练习册和CD-ROM盘一张）

未经许可，不得以任何方式复制或抄袭本书之部分或全部内容。
版权所有，侵权必究
举报电话：（010）62752024
电子信箱：fd@pup.pku.edu.cn

前言

《双双中文教材》是一套专门为海外青少年编写的中文课本，是我在美国八年的中文教学实践基础上编写成的。在介绍这套教材之前，请读一首小诗：

> 一双神奇的手，
> 推开一扇窗。
> 一条神奇的路，
> 通向灿烂的中华文化。
>
> 鲍凯文 鲍维江
> 1998年

鲍维江和鲍凯文姐弟俩是美国生美国长的孩子，也是我的学生。1998年冬，他们送给我的新年贺卡上的小诗，深深地打动了我的心。我把这首诗看成我文化教学的"回声"。我要传达给海外每位中文老师：我教给他们（学生）中国文化，他们思考了、接受了、回应了。这条路走通了！

语言是交际的工具，更是一种文化和一种生活方式，所以学习中文也就离不开中华文化的学习。汉字是一种古老的象形文字，她从远古走来，带有大量的文化信息，但学起来并不容易。使学生增强兴趣、减小难度，走出苦学汉字的怪圈，走进领悟中华文化的花园，是我编写这套教材的初衷。

学生不论大小，天生都有求知的欲望，都有欣赏文化美的追求。中华文化本身是魅力十足的。把这宏大而玄妙的文化，深入浅出地，有声有色地介绍出来，让这迷人的文化如涓涓细流，一点一滴地渗入学生们的心田，使学生们逐步体味中国文化，是我编写这套教材的目的。

为此我将汉字的学习放入文化介绍的流程之中同步进行，让同学们在学中国地理的同时，学习汉字；在学中国历史的同时，学习汉字；在学中国哲学的同时，学习汉字；在学中国科普文选的同时，学习汉字……

这样的一种中文学习，知识性强，趣味性强；老师易教，学生易学。当学生们合上书本时，他们的眼前是中国的大好河山，是中国五千年的历史和妙不可言的哲学思维，是奔腾的现代中国……

总之，他们了解了中华文化，就会探索这片土地，热爱这片土地，就会与中国结下情缘。

最后我要衷心地感谢所有热情支持和帮助我编写教材的老师、家长、学生、朋友和家人，特别是老同学唐玲教授、何茜老师、我姐姐王欣欣编审及我女儿Uta Guo年复一年的鼎力相助。可以说这套教材是大家努力的结果。

王双双
2005年5月8日

说明

《双双中文教材》是一套专门为海外学生编写的中文教材。它是由美国加州王双双老师和中国专家学者共同努力，在海外多年的实践中编写出来的。全书共20册，识字量2500个，包括了从识字、拼音、句型、短文的学习，到初步的较系统的中国文化的学习。教材大体介绍了中国地理、历史、哲学等方面的丰富内容，突出了中国文化的魅力。课本知识面广，趣味性强，深入浅出，易教易学。

这套教材体系完整、构架灵活、使用面广。学生可以从零起点开始，一直学完全部课程20册；也可以将后11册（10～20册）的九个文化专题和第五册（汉语拼音）单独使用，这样便于高中和大学开设中国哲学、地理、历史等专门课程以及假期班、短期中国文化班、拼音速成班使用，符合了美国AP中文课程的目标和基本要求。

这本《中国古代哲学》是《双双中文教材》的第十八册，由王双双在陈战国先生（北京社会科学院哲学所所长）的指导和帮助下，经过多年的努力，在海外中文教学实践的基础上编写而成。全书以简单的语言，将中国古代先秦哲学伦理思想作了概括介绍。通过对本书的学习，学生将会基本了解中国古代儒、道两家的思想，不仅能提高中文水平，也能提高思辨能力，从而可以在思想的层面上领略中华文化的精妙之处。

这里还要特别鸣谢曹儒伯先生在英文翻译上给予的帮助。

编者

课程设置

一年级	中文课本(第一册)	中文课本(第二册)	中文课本(第三册)
二年级	中文课本(第四册)	中文课本(第五册)	中文课本(第六册)
三年级	中文课本(第七册)	中文课本(第八册)	中文课本(第九册)
四年级	中国成语故事	中国地理常识	
五年级	中国古代故事	中国神话传说	
六年级	中国古代科学技术	中国文学欣赏	
七年级	中国诗歌欣赏	中文科普阅读	
八年级	中国古代哲学	中国历史(上)	
九年级	中国历史(下)	小说阅读，中文SAT II	
十年级	中文SAT II (强化班)	小说阅读，中文SAT II 考试	

目录

第一课	孔子的思想	1
第二课	孟子的思想	11
第三课	荀子的思想	20
第四课	墨子的思想	29
第五课	老子的思想	38
第六课	庄子的思想	48
第七课	孙子的思想	58
第八课	《易经》的思想	67
生字表		75
生词表		77

第一课

孔子的思想

孔子（前551—前479）是中国伟大的思想家、教育家。他与古希腊的苏格拉底、印度的释迦牟尼(jiā móu)生活在同一时代，是中国的圣人。他的思想对于中国和世界都有很大的影响。他创立了儒家学派。

孔子一生都在努力教导人们如何做人，如何做有道德的人。他告诉人们，做一个道德高尚的人必须做到以下几点：

孔子像

一、"爱人"。有一个学生问孔子什么是"仁"？他解释说："爱人。""仁"指最高尚的道德品质，也指有高尚道德品质的人。孔子认为，人最根本、最高尚的品质就是爱人。一个人只有能够爱别人，才是一个有道德的人。爱人要真诚，而不能虚情假意。爱人首先是爱自己的父母、爱自己的兄弟姐妹、爱自己的朋友，因为这些人与你天天生活在一起，和你最有感情。从自己的亲人爱起，从自己身边的人爱起，一直到爱所有的人，爱所有的物，爱整个宇宙。

真诚地爱自己的亲人容易，真诚地爱一切人、一切物很难。一个人总有他喜欢的人，也有他不喜欢的人；总有他喜欢的物，也有他不喜欢的物。要想做到爱一切人和一切物，就必须有很高的精神境界，把整个世界看成是一个大家庭。中国宋朝有一个叫张载的人说过，天是父亲，地是母亲，所有的人都是我的兄弟姐妹，所有的物都是我的同类。当时还有一个叫程颢（hào）的人说，整个宇宙是一个大生命，宇宙间的一切东西都是血肉相连的，这种血肉相连的关系就是"仁"，割断了这种关系就是"不仁"。一个人只有把自己放入整个宇宙之中，只有像爱自己的生命一样地去爱宇宙中的一切，才是一个有最高道德品质的人。他们的这些思想都是从孔子的思想中发展出来的。

二、"忠恕"。"忠"是尽心尽力地帮助别人，"恕"是对别人要宽容。孔子说"己欲立而立人，己欲达而达人"，"己所不欲，勿施于人"。人都希望得到幸福、快乐和事业上的成功，都不希望遭到不幸、痛苦和失败。因此，一个有道德的人就应该帮助别人得到幸福、快乐和成功，帮助别人免遭不幸、痛苦和失败。自己希望得到的，应该帮助别人也得到；自己不愿意遇到的情况，也应该帮助别人不要遇到；希望别人怎么对自己，自己也应该怎么去对别人。这一做人的原则，叫做"忠恕之道"。

三、"克己复礼"。"克己"就是克制自己的私欲，约束自己的行为；"复礼"就是遵守各种社会规范。为了使社会稳定，人们定出了许多规范，用来约束人们的行为。一个有道德的人，就要自觉地遵守各种社会规范，做对社会有益的事，不要破坏社会秩序。

孔子教人怎么做人的思想很丰富，以上三点是最重要的。人们只要努力按照这三点去做，就一定能够成为一个道德高尚的人。

王金泰 画

中国古代哲学

生词

jiào yù	教育	education
xī là	希腊	Greek
rú jiā	儒家	Confucianism
xué pài	学派	school
dào dé	道德	morality
gāo shàng	高尚	noble
jiě shì	解释	explanation
gǎn qíng	感情	emotion
jīng shén jìng jiè	精神境界	spiritual ethos; mental outlook
gē duàn	割断	cut off
zhōng shù	忠恕	loyalty and forbearance
kuān róng	宽容	tolerant
shī	施	bestow; grant
shì yè	事业	career
kè zhì	克制	refrain
yuē shù	约束	control
xíng wéi	行为	behaviour
zūn shǒu	遵守	abide by; observe
guī fàn	规范	rules and norms
wěn dìng	稳定	stable
zhì xù	秩序	order

听写

感情　道德　教育　遵守　稳定　解释　行为　高尚

秩序　割断　*施　忠恕

注：*号以后的字词为选做题，后同。

比一比

创 { 创造 / 创立　　克 { 克制 / 克服　　派 { 学派 / 派人　　尚 { 高尚 / 和尚

束 { 约束 / 结束　　境 { 境界 / 环境　　序 { 秩序 / 顺序　　范 { 规范 / 范围

字词运用

遵守　　尊敬

要遵守交通规则，不要闯红灯。

我们要尊敬老人。

品质

热心帮助别人是一种好品质。

哥哥不仅学习好，品质也好。

近义词

有益——有利

反义词

真诚——虚伪　　　　　　有益——有害

根据课文回答问题

1. 孔子是什么时期的人？

2. 孔子创立了什么学派？

3. 请解释孔子"仁"、"忠"、"恕"的思想。

4. 请解释孔子的"爱人"的思想和"忠恕之道"。

5. 什么是"己欲立而立人，己欲达而达人"，"己所不欲，勿施于人"？

词语解释

有益——有好处；有帮助。

真诚——真心实意，没有一点虚假。

创立——初次建立。

免遭——避免遇到。

虚情假意——对人的感情不是真心的，而是假装出来的。

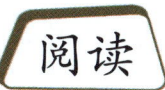

阅读

孔子简介

孔子，名丘，字仲尼，春秋时期鲁国人，著名的教育家、思想家，儒家学派的创始人。孔子曾代理鲁国宰相，后周游列国，推行自己的政治主张，但都没有成功。他晚年整理古代文化典籍，编订了"六经"[①]等书，对中国文化发展贡献极大。

孔子好学

孔子从小十分好学，学习上有了问题就向人请教，一定要弄明白。孔子学习不仅仅要学会，还要做到精益求精。

有一次他跟老师学琴。一支曲子学了十几天，老师很满意地说："弹得不错，可以学新曲子了。"孔子却不满意，说："曲子我会弹了，但弹得不熟。"过了几天，孔子已经弹得流畅动听了，但他还不满意，对老师说："这支曲子的神韵我还没领会，让我再练习几天吧。"又过了几天，老师说："现在你弹得完美无缺，可见你已经领会曲子的韵味了。咱们练习新曲子吧。"可孔子却说："我还没有体会出作曲者是谁，他是个什么样的人呢！"接着又埋头弹起来。直到有一天，孔子跑到老师面前，兴奋地说：

[①] "六经"包括《诗》《书》《礼》《易》《春秋》和《乐》。

"我已经能从曲子中感受到作曲者的形象了:他脸黑黑的,个子高高的,眼睛炯炯有神地望着远方,四面八方的国家都臣服于他。除了周文王,这个人还会是谁呢?"老师听了十分佩服,站起来行礼说:"哎呀,你真了不起!我的老师教我这支曲子时,就说曲名叫《文王操》。"

孔子是多么富有钻研精神啊!

问题

孔子跟老师学琴时,为什么要反复练习一支曲子而不学习新曲子呢?

生词

zhòng ní 仲尼	Zhongni (another name of confucius)	liú chàng 流畅	smooth
zhǔ zhāng 主张	view; proposition	shén yùn 神韵	romantic charm
biān dìng 编订	compile	wán měi wú quē 完美无缺	perfect
jīng yì qiú jīng 精益求精	constantly perfect one's skill	lǐng huì 领会	understand
qǔ diào 曲调	tune; melody	jiǒng jiǒng yǒu shén 炯炯有神	(of eyes) bright and piercing
		zuān yán 钻研	study

Lesson One

Confucius Thought

Confucius (551 B.C.—479 B.C.), is a great Chinese thinker and educator. He is a Chinese saint, a contemporary of the Greek Socrates and Indian Sankyamuni. His philosophy and thoughts have exerted great influence not only in China, but the entire world as well. The philosophy he established is called Confucianism.

Throughout his life, Confucius made a substantial effort to educate people on how to be a good and moral person. He told them to be a person with high moral virtue must be able to achieve the following.

First, "Love People": When asked by a student what is "benevolence (*Ren*)", Confucius replied that it is "loving people." "Benevolence" implies the highest morality. In his opinion, the most basic and highest moral of mankind is to love people. Only a person who can love others can be considered moral. Loving people must be sincere and can't be fake or pretending. Loving people is that first love one's parents, brothers and sisters, and your friends and relatives, because these people are living with you every day and know you most intimately. Beginning with your immediate family members, you should spread your love from people around you to all people and all things, including the entire universe.

It's easy to love your own immediate family members sincerely, but truly loving anybody or anything would be difficult. One always has his own likes and dislikes. It calls for a sublime spirit and state to love all people and all things, regarding the whole world as a big family. Zhang Zai in the Song Dynasty described it as "Heaven is father, Earth is mother, all people are my brothers and sisters and all things are of my kind." Cheng Hao, who lived at the same time, said, "The whole universe is a big life, in which everything is connected as close as flesh and blood. Such a connection is called 'Benevolence' and it is 'not benevolent' if we eliminate such a connection. Only a person who immerses himself in the whole universe and loves everything as much as his life can possess the highest morality." All their thoughts originated from Confucian ideals.

Second, "loyalty and forbearance": "Loyalty (*Zhong*)" means trying one's best to help others while "forbearance (*Shu*)" implies being lenient and tolerant of others. Confucius stated, "Desiring to sustain oneself, one sustains; desiring to develop oneself, one develops others", and "Do not do to others what you do not wish yourself." Everyone hopes to be happy, joyful and successful instead of being unfortunate, suffering and a failure. Therefore, a person with morality should help others obtain happiness, joy and success, and avoid misfortune, suffering and failure. If one hopes to receive, they should help others receive and avoid what one doesn't want; I will treat others as others treat me. This is the principle of mankind and in China is called "the Principle of Loyalty and Forbearance".

Third, "to exercise self-restraint and return to propriety": "To exercise self-restraint (*Keji*)" implies restraining one's own desire and controlling one's behavior; "To return to propriety (*Fuli*)" is to follow all social rules and boundaries. To achieve a stable society, man has established rules and boundaries to control people's behavior. A person with morality should be able to consciously follow all social conventions, bringing benefit to the society instead of social disorder.

Confucius provided a wealth of thoughts in teaching people how to be a man; the three principles above were the most important. If people follow these three principles and try their best, they are sure to be of virtue.

A Brief Introduction to Confucius

Confucius, whose real name is Kong Qiu with a cognomen Zhongni, was born in the state of Lu during the Spring and Autumn period. He was known as a famous educator, thinker and was the founder of Confucianism. He once was the acting minister of Lu and later visited many other states throughout his life, trying to carry out his political ideas, but all in vain. But as a great contributor to the development of Chinese culture, he collected the ancient classics, compiled and edited several valuable books such as the *Six Disciplines*[1] in his later years.

Confucius' Persistence with Learning

Ever since a little boy, Confucius was very fond of learning. Whenever he met difficult questions, he would ask help from the others until he understood the answers clearly. Not only did he try to acquire knowledge, but he also aimed to be the best.

He once learned to play *Guqin* from a teacher. After he practiced one piece of music for about ten days, his teacher said satisfactorily, "you've done a good job and you may start to learn a new one". But Confucius was not satisfied, saying "I mastered the tone, but the skills still desire to be improved." A few days later, the music Confucius played was very pleasant to the ear. However, Confucius was still not satisfied, telling the teacher that "I still cannot get the spirit of this music, so please allow me a few more days to practice." Several days passed and the teacher suggested, "Now you played it perfectly and we may practice a new one since you have already mastered the spirit". Confucius answered, "I haven't come to visualize who the composer is and what he is like." Then he began to play *Guqin* again wholeheartedly. He played the same music for many days until one day, he ran to the teacher with great excitement, "I can imagine who the composer is: he is tall with a swarthy complexion and a pair of gleaming and penetrating eyes. He is looking into the distance, all the states around acknowledging allegiance to him. Who else could it be except for Wen Wang (the ruler of Zhou)?" Hearing this, the teacher admired him so much that he bowed to Confucius, exclaiming "Wow, you are so great! My teacher told me it was indeed titled 'Wen Wang Cao'."

From this, we can see how intensely Confucius was absorbed in learning.

---

1 *Six Disciplines* are *Shi* (the Books of Odes), *Shu* (the Books of History), *Li* (the Books of Rites), *Yi* (the Books of Changes), *Chunqiu* (the Books of Spring and Autumn Annals), and *Yue* (the Books of Music).

第二课

孟子的思想

孟子像

孟子（前372—前289）是中国重要的哲学家、思想家，是孔子思想的主要继承人之一，被中国人尊称为"亚圣"（第二圣人）。他主要继承了孔子"仁者爱人"的思想，对人为什么有道德，为什么会爱人的问题做了理论上的说明。

一、"四端"。孔子说，人应该有道德，应该爱人。人为什么会有道德？为什么会爱人呢？孟子回答说，因为人有"四端"。"端"是起点、开始的意思。孟子说的"四端"，是指道德的四个起点。这四个起点是"恻隐之心"、"羞恶(wù)之心"、"辞让之心"、"是非之心"。"恻隐之心"就是同情心；"羞恶之心"就是做了错事、坏事会感到羞耻；"辞让之心"就是懂得谦让；"是非之心"就是能分别对错和善恶。孟子认为"四端"是人生来就有的，是人与其他动物的根本区别。"四端"发展起来，就会成为四种美德："恻隐之心"会发展成为爱人（仁），"羞恶之心"会发展成为正义

（义①），"辞让之心"会发展成为有礼貌（礼），"是非之心"会发展成为明善恶（智）。

这四种"心"怎样才能顺利地发展起来呢？孟子说："心勿忘，勿助长。""勿忘"就是不要忘记它们，要像对待幼苗那样爱护它们。"勿助长"就是不要急于求成。孟子讲过一个故事：一个农民栽了一片禾苗，第二天他见禾苗没有长高，心里有些着急。第三天见禾苗还没有长高，心里更着急了，于是他就把禾苗一棵一棵地都拔高了一点。到了第四天，所有的禾苗都死了。这就是"拔苗助长"的故事。人的道德品质是逐渐培养起来的，既要不间断地努力，又不要拔苗助长。

二、"仁政"。和孔子一样，孟子也认为在各种美德中"爱人"是最重要、最根本的。只有能真心爱人的人，对别人有一颗爱心的人，才是真正有道德的人。一个国家的领导人更需要有这样的道德，他必须对人民有一颗爱心。国家的领导人应该"老吾老以及人之老，幼吾幼以及人之幼"。意思是说，国家领导人爱自己的父亲和母亲，也要爱别人的父亲和母亲；爱自己的妻子和儿女，也要爱别人的

---

① 孟子说的"义"是指行为正当，符合道德规范，与通常说的"正义"意思不完全相同。

妻子和儿女。自己想生活得幸福快乐，也要让所有的人都能生活得幸福快乐。人民是国家的基础，只有爱人民的人才能得到人民的拥护和爱戴，只有得到了人民的拥护和爱戴才有资格当国家的领导人。用一颗爱人之心去管理国家就叫做"仁政"。

生词

lǐ lùn 理论	theory	duì dài 对待	treat
cè yǐn 恻隐	compassion	zāi 栽	plant; grow
tóng qíng 同情	sympathize with	péi yǎng 培养	develop; foster
xiū chǐ 羞耻	shame	gēn běn 根本	essential; core
qiān ràng 谦让	modesty	lǐng dǎo 领导	leader
shàn è 善恶	good and evil	rén mín 人民	people
qū bié 区别	distinguish	yōng hù 拥护	advocate; support
zhèng yì 正义	righteous	ài dài 爱戴	adore; hold in high esteem
shùn lì 顺利	smoothly; favorably	zī gé 资格	qualification

听写

对待　理论　人民　顺利　领导　同情　善恶　正义

栽　培养　*端　羞耻

比一比

羞 { 羞耻 / 羞恶 }　　顺 { 顺利 / 顺序 }　　待 { 对待 / 等待 }　　资 { 资格 / 资源 }

养 { 培养 / 营养 }　　非 { 是非 / 非常 }　　德 { 道德 / 德国 }　　护 { 拥护 / 保护 }

字词运用

同情

诗歌《卖炭翁》表达了白居易对穷人的同情。

奶奶是一个很有同情心的人，别人有困难她总是帮忙。

爱护

我们班的同学都很爱护公共财物。

老师告诉我们要爱护动物。

人类要爱护自然环境。

说明

你总把三看成五,说明你很粗心。

你迟到了,请说明原因。

对待

对待朋友要真诚,不能虚情假意。

多音字

间 jiàn

不间断 jiàn

间 jiān

一间房 jiān

根据课文回答问题

1. 孟子是什么时期的人?

2. 为什么称孟子为"亚圣"?

3. 请解释孟子思想中"四端"的意思:"恻隐之心"、"羞恶之心"、"辞让之心"、"是非之心"。

4. 什么是"心勿忘,勿助长"?

词语解释

是非——正确与错误，善与恶。

爱护——爱惜并保护。

间断——中间断开，不连接；不连续。

急于求成——想要马上就实现或马上就成功。

说明——解释明白；解释意义的话；证明。

阅读

孟子简介

孟子名轲(kē)，战国时期鲁国人，中国重要的哲学家、思想家，是孔子思想的主要继承人之一。

孟母教子

孟子小的时候，并不爱学习。他成天跑到离家不远的一个墓地去玩，学着挖坑埋葬死人，有时连饭都忘了回家吃。于是孟母决定搬家，以免儿子再到墓地去玩。孟母把家搬到街市的附近去住，但是没想到，孟子又跟着商人上街去学着叫卖。孟母发现后，觉得这个住处也不好。最后孟母把家搬到一所学堂旁边，孟子便开始进学堂读书了。

孟子虽然上了学堂读书，但是并不努力，不专心，很贪玩，经常迟到早退，使母亲很担忧。一天，孟母正在家中织布，又见

到孟子很早就从学堂跑回了家。孟母问道:"你为什么回来这么早?"孟子撒谎说:"不早,跟平时一样呀!"孟母听完儿子的回答非常痛心,便拿起剪刀,把织布机上的纱线一下子剪断,再也不说什么,只坐在一旁落泪。孟子见到这种情景,内心十分难过。这时,孟母语重心长地对儿子说:"要你好好读书,是希望你能成才。像你现在这样,总是还没到放学的时候就不学了,这不就等于剪断纱线,让我织不成布吗?"孟子听完母亲的话,眼泪直流。他从此努力学习,终于成为"亚圣"。

王金泰 画

生词

xué táng 学堂	school	shā xiàn 纱线	yarn
tān wán 贪玩	addicted to playing	yǔ zhòng xīn cháng 语重心长	(to say sth.) with great concern or in all earnestness
zǎo tuì 早退	leave early		
sā huǎng 撒谎	tell a lie	děng yú 等于	be equal to; the same as

Lesson Two
Mencius Thought

Mencius (372B.C.—289B.C.), an important philosopher, thinker, Confucianism's main follower, was honored as "the Junior Sage" (the Second Saint) in China. He mainly inherited Confucianism, "benevolence consists in loving people", and made a theoretical elaboration of Confucius' thought, by explaining why individuals should be moral and why people should love others.

First, "Four Beginnings (*Siduan*)": Confucius said that people should be moral and love others, but one may wonder why they should be moral and love others. In Mencius' opinion, all men in their original nature possess "Four Beginnings (*Siduan*)". "*Duan*" means the starting point or the beginning. Here what Mencius meant "four beginnings" refer to the four moral principles: the feelings of "commiseration", "shame and dislike", "modesty and yielding", "right and wrong". "The feeling of commiseration" means being sympathetic; "The feeling of shame and dislike" means feeling shameful after something is done wrong or bad; "The feeling of modesty and yielding" means knowing how to be polite; "the feeling of right and wrong" means distinguishing right from wrong, and good from bad. Mencius believed that man is born with these "four beginnings", as a fundamental difference between human and the other animals. These "four beginnings" could be developed into four constant virtues: "The feeling of commiseration" can enable people to love others (which can be called "*Ren*"—benevolence); "The feeling of shame and dislike" can make people righteous (that is "*Yi*"[1]—righteousness); "The feeling of modesty and yielding" could become politeness (it is called "*Li*"—propriety), and "the feeling of right and wrong" could become an ability to distinguish good versus evil (that is "*Zhi*"—wisdom).

However, how could these four feelings be developed smoothly? Mencius suggested, "Never forget; never hasten." "Never forget" means people should keep these feelings in mind and care for them like cherishing seedlings; and "Never hasten" implies people should not attempt to desire for a quick success. It is put in such a story told by Mencius: a farmer once planted some seedlings in a rice field. The next day he was worried when he didn't find the seedlings growing taller. The third day he still didn't see any seedling growth, and became extremely anxious, so the farmer pulled the seedlings one by one up a little. On the fourth day, all the seedlings died. This is the story of "*ba miao zhu zhang*", which implies that the qualities of one's virtues are developed gradually, not only requiring non-stop effort, but also avoiding activities that might rush results and have an adverse outcome.

Second, "Benevolent Governance (*Renzheng*)": Same as Confucius, Mencius also held that "loving people" is the most important and basic one among all. Only those with a heart of sincere love and

---

1 "*Yi*" mentioned here by Mencius refers to proper behaviors which usually conform to moral standards, different from "being righteous" in conventional sense.

kindness are people with true moral principles. A nation's leaders require more of this type of virtue and must have a loving heart for their people. A nation's leaders should "treat the aged in your family as they should be treated, and extend this treatment to the aged of other people's families; treat the young in your family as they should be treated, and extend this treatment to the young of other people's families". This principle means that the leaders should love his people's parents, wives, sons and daughters as much as his own parents, wife, sons and daughters. Only those who can make all the other people happy will be truly living a happy life. Since people are the foundation of a nation, only those who love their people will receive people's support and love, and only those who receive people's support and love have the qualifications to be the nation's leader. Therefore, the way to govern a nation with a loving heart is called "Benevolent Governance".

A Brief Introduction to Mencius

Mencius, whose original name is Meng Ke, was born in the state of Lu during the Warring States period. He was known as an important Chinese philosopher and thinker, one of the main followers of Confucian thought.

Mencius' Mother Educating Her Son

When Mencius was a little boy, he didn't love to study at all. All day he went to play at a cemetery nearby his home and learned how to dig holes to bury the dead, sometimes even forgetting to go back home for meals. Therefore, Mencius' mother decided to move to prevent her son from playing in the cemetery. She moved their home near a market. Unexpectedly, Mencius went to the market, following some merchants to learn how to hawk their wares. After Mencius' mother knew of this, she didn't feel the market was a good place to educate her child. Finally, Mencius' mother moved into a place close to a school, where Mencius started going to school to study.

Although Mencius was sent for schooling, he still didn't study hard, didn't focus and was addicted to playing, frequently going to school late and leaving school early, which worried his mother a lot. One day, when Mencius mother was weaving cloth at home, Mencius came back from school earlier than usual. She asked him "why did you come back so early?" Mencius lied, "Not early, just the same as usual." Hearing the words, Mencius' mother felt so heart-broken that she took up a pair of scissors and angrily cut off the thread on the weaving machine, sitting beside, with tears in eyes, speechless. Seeing this, Mencius was very upset. After a while, his mother said to him with great concern, "My son, I wish you would study hard because I wish you would become a useful person. But if you just act like this, often quitting before school dismissal, isn't it the same as my cutting the thread and never able to finish weaving the cloth?" Mencius heard his mother's words, tears running down his cheeks and thereafter he studied very hard and became "the Junior Sage" in the end.

第三课

荀子的思想

荀子（约前313—前238）是中国重要的思想家、哲学家，孔子思想的主要继承人之一。他和孟子虽然都是孔子思想的继承者，但他的思想却与孟子的思想有很大的区别。

荀子像

一、性恶论。孔子没有明确说过人性是善还是恶，他认为人的本性并没有太大的差别，不同的习惯才使人与人之间出现了差别。孟子认为人生来就有"四端"，"四端"发展起来就成了四种美德，这叫做"性善论"。荀子认为孟子的说法是不对的，他说："人之性，恶；其善者，伪也。""伪"就是人为的努力。为什么这样说呢？因为人生来就有各种欲望，就有为自己求利益的本能，这些本能就是人性。如果顺着这些本能发展下去，人与人之间就会发生争斗，所以说人性是恶的。不过人能学习，能接受教育，通过学习和接受教育就会具有道德。因此，治

理国家不能只靠一颗爱心，而要制定完善的制度和法规。

二、"明于天人之分"。"天"就是自然界。"明于天人之分"就是分清什么是自然界的性质和功能，什么是人的性质和功能。荀子认为，自然界是运动变化的、有规律的，它的运动变化并没有什么目的，也不会按照人的愿望去改变。它的功能就是使万物自然地生长。自然界中的各种事物都相互联系、相互依靠，每一种事物都以其他事物为营养，它自己又是其他事物的营养。

人虽然也是自然界中的一种物，但人要比其他的自然物更有力量。人不是生来就有道德的，但人生来就有理性。人的理性分为两个方面：一个方面是人能认识自然、利用自然、改造自然。人不长毛，不能御寒，但人会织布，会做衣服；人没有锋利的爪牙，但人能制造和使用武器；人的力量小，走路慢，但人能制造车船。另一方面是人能组织成群体，组织成社会，能利用集体的力量战胜其他事物。有了这两点，人就成了世界上最伟大的事物了。

人虽然能认识自然、利用自然、改造自然，但是人的力量并不是无限的。人应该认识到什么是人力能做到的，什么是受自然规律控制的、人力改变不了的。人应该努力发挥自己的能力去认识世界和改造世界，但是不要企图认

识自己不能认识的东西，不要企图改变自己不能改变的东西，这就叫做"明于天人之分"。

生词

荀子 xún zǐ	Xun Zi (name)	依靠 yī kào	rely on
伪 wěi	hypocritical; counterfeit	改造 gǎi zào	reform
具有 jù yǒu	have; possess	御寒 yù hán	keep out the cold
制度 zhì dù	regulation; rule	锋利 fēng lì	sharp
性质 xìng zhì	nature	组织 zǔ zhī	organize
功能 gōng néng	function	社会 shè huì	society
规律 guī lù	law	集体 jí tǐ	collective
目的 mù dì	aim; purpose	发挥 fā huī	exert
联系 lián xì	connection	企图 qǐ tú	attempt

听写

联系　依靠　改造　社会　组织　制度　目的　规律

具有　*企图　发挥

比一比

规 { 法规 / 规律

能 { 能力 / 功能

制 { 制度 / 制造

具 { 具有 / 工具

质 { 性质 / 品质

改 { 改造 / 改变

组 { 组织 / 小组

企 { 企图 / 企鹅

挥 { 发挥 / 挥手

字词运用

规律　　法规

水在零度结冰是自然规律。

他每天早上七点起床,晚上十点睡觉,生活很有规律。

学开车一定要先学交通法规。

制度　　制造

要遵守学校的制度,上课不迟到。

这辆车是中国制造的。

联系

请你一定回个信，不然咱们就会失去联系。

这是我的电话号码(mǎ)，有事请与我联系。

目的

你知道他这样做有什么目的吗？

近义词

区别——辨别　　　　　企图——打算

反义词

真——伪　　　　　　　集体——个人

多音字

的(de)　　　　　　　　的(dì)
我的(de)　　　　　　　目的(dì)

根据课文回答问题

1. 荀子是什么时期的哲学家?

2. 荀子"性恶论"的内容是什么?

3. 孟子"性善论"的内容是什么?

4. 请解释荀子"明于天人之分"的观点。

相配词语连线

战胜　　　　教育

接受　　　　高尚

制定　　　　秩序

品德　　　　敌人

破坏　　　　法规

阅读

荀子简介

荀子名况,战国末期赵国人,中国古代重要的思想家之一。荀子认为人性本恶,必须用礼仪、刑罚来约束人的行为。他还认为自然界有它自己的运行规律。他著有《荀子》一书。

中国古代哲学

《荀子·劝学》选读

（一）锲而不舍

良马跳跃一下，达不到十步远；劣马拉十天车却能走很远的路程，这是不停地走的结果。雕刻一样东西，用刀子刻几下就停止，朽木也刻不断；不停地刻下去，才能将金石雕刻成器。这说明只有坚持下去，有恒心，才能把事情做成功。

（二）不积跬步，无以至千里；不积细流，无以成江海

如果走路不一步一步地积累，就不能达到千里之远；不汇集细小的水流，就不能成为江海。这说明学习必须一点一点地积累，也说明事情的成功都是由小到大逐渐积累的。

生词

xíng fá 刑罚	punishment	xiǔ mù 朽木	rotten wood
qiè ér bù shě 锲而不舍	work with persistence	jiān chí 坚持	insist on; stick to
tiào yuè 跳跃	jump; leap; gallop	kuǐ bù 跬步	half a step; small or short step
diāo kè 雕刻	carve	jī lěi 积累	accumulate

Lesson Three

Thought of Xun Zi

Xun Zi (about 313 B.C.—238 B.C.), an important thinker and philosopher in China, was also one of the main followers of Confucian thought, but his thought is quite different from Mencius' thought. They are mainly listed as follows:

First, "The Evilness of Human Nature": Confucius, not clearly explaining whether human nature is good or evil, believed that there was no big difference among human nature and only different habits distinguish one from the other; while Mencius believed that man is born with "Four Beginnings", which can be developed into four virtues. It is called "the goodness of human nature". However, Xun Zi didn't agree with Mencius by saying that "the nature of man is evil; his goodness is acquired by training". Here "*wei*" means the acquired. Why did he say such words? In his opinion, man is born with various inherent desires and instincts for one's own profit. These instincts are human nature. If led by these instincts, people would fall into fight with each other, so human nature is evil. However, man can learn and get educated, gradually becoming a person with moral principles. Thus, it is not enough to govern a nation merely with a heart of love, sound and complete rules and policies should be established.

Second, "A distinction being made between Heaven and Man". Here "*tian* (heaven)" refers to the Nature. This theory means it should be clarified that what is the nature and function of Nature and what is the nature and function of Man. Xun Zi holds that the Nature is moving and changing according to its own objective laws, without any particular purpose, and independent of man's will. Its function is to help all things grow naturally. Everything in the Nature is inter-related and co-dependent, feeding the others and fed by the others.

Man, as one existence among the Nature, is more powerful than other existences, because he is not born with morality but with rationality. His rationality has two aspects: one aspect is his ability to know the Nature, use the Nature and reform the Nature. Man can weave cloth to make clothes against the cold although his body does not grow feathers; man can make and use the weapons for protection although he has no sharp claws; man can make ship and vehicles for travel although he is comparatively weak and walks slowly. Another aspect is man's ability to organize people into groups and form a society to overcome the other difficulties. Thus, with these two aspects man becomes the greatest in the world.

However, man's power is not limitless although man can know the Nature, use the Nature and reform the Nature. Man should know what can be accomplished by human's effort and what is under the control of the natural laws beyond human's power. Man should exert his own effort and try to know and reform the Nature, but not attempt to know what he can't know or change something that is beyond his ability. This is the essence of so-called "A distinction being made between Heaven and Man".

中国古代哲学

A Brief Introduction to Xun Zi

Xun Zi, whose original name is Xun Kuang, was born in the state of Zhao in the end period of Warring States. He was one of the most important thinkers in ancient China. Xun Zi believed that human nature is evil, so man's behaviors should be kept within certain bounds by rituals and punishment. In addition, he held that the Nature has its own laws of movement. All of these ideas are recorded in his monograph titled *Xun Zi*.

Excerpts from *On Study* in *Xun Zi*

1. To Work with Perseverance

Even a strong horse cannot gallop far more than ten strides, but a weak horse can cover a long distance if it keeps on dragging the cart for ten days. The continuous effort makes the difference. When carved, with only a few times, even rotten wood cannot be cut down, but metal and stone can be carved into different shapes with non-stop chiseling. It reveals the truth that success will come to you as long as you stick to what you want with perseverance.

2. A Thousand *Li* are Covered Step by Step; Rivers and Seas are Formed by A Thousand Streams

You won't reach as far as a thousand *li,* if you don't continue walking step by step; there won't be any river or sea, if a thousand streams do not flow and merge together. Such facts reveal the truth that knowledge is obtained through gradual effort and success is achieved by accumulated small gains.

第四课

墨子的思想

墨子（约前475—前396）是中国重要的思想家、哲学家。他创立了墨家学派。墨子和他的学生大多数是手工业者，他们都很重视劳动和劳动成果，经常讨论劳动问题。墨子认为，人与其他的动物不同。其他的动物以身上长的毛为衣服，以蹄爪为鞋子，以自然

墨子像

的水草为饮料和饭菜，所以它们不用劳动就能生存。人是不同的，人必须通过劳动才能有衣服穿、有饭菜吃，通过劳动才能生存，因此每一个人都应该劳动。一个人到别人的果园里去偷水果，这样的行为对不对呢？当然是不对的，因为他没有劳动而占有别人的劳动成果。人只有参加劳动才能享受劳动成果，不劳而获是不道德的。

一、"兼相爱"。"兼相爱"就是人与人之间互相爱。墨子也认为人的最高道德是爱人，但他说的爱人和孔子、孟

子所说的爱人不一样。孔子、孟子所说的爱人是一种有差别的爱。他们主张要先爱自己的父母，再爱别人的父母；先爱自己的亲人，再爱别人的亲人；爱自己的父母要比爱别人的父母多一些，爱自己的亲人要比爱别人的亲人多一些。这叫做"爱有差等"。墨子主张爱人不应该有差别，爱别人的国家就像爱自己的国家一样，爱别人的父母就像爱自己的父母一样，爱别人就像爱自己一样。爱人应该从自己做起，自己要先去爱别人，别人才会爱自己；自己要先去爱别人的父母，别人才会爱自己的父母；自己要先去爱别人的国家，别人才会爱自己的国家。如果人与人之间，家与家之间，国与国之间都能互相爱，世界上就没有争夺，没有战争了。

二、"交相利"。"交相利"就是互利。墨子认为，判断一个人的行为是不是道德的，不仅要看他的行为动机，还要看他的行为效果。只有以爱人为动机并且能给人带来实际利益的行为才是有道德的行为。因此他认为"兼相爱"应该体现在"交相利"上，就是体现为人与人之间的互利。墨子主张，人与人之间要互相帮助，强壮的人要帮助弱小的人，富人要帮助穷人，有知识的人要帮助没有知识的人，要让那些没有妻子儿女的老人和失去了父母的孤儿有所依靠，要让所有的人都能过上好生活。无论是国家还是个人，以大欺小，以强欺弱，以富欺贫都是不道德的。

生词

chéng guǒ 成果 achievement	zhēng duó 争夺 fight for
tǎo lùn 讨论 discuss	hù lì 互利 mutual benefit
yǐn liào 饮料 drinks; beverages	dòng jī 动机 motivation
shēng cún 生存 survive	xiào guǒ 效果 effect
zhàn yǒu 占有 own; possess	tǐ xiàn 体现 embody; represent
xiǎng shòu 享受 enjoy	zhǔ zhāng 主张 advocate; proposition
jiān 兼 simultaneously; concurrently	

听写

主张　生存　享受　饮料　体现　互利　动机　讨论

效果　成果　*争夺　兼

比一比

存 { 生存 / 存在 }   动 { 动机 / 运动 }   现 { 发现 / 体现 }

果 { 效果 / 成果 }   饮 { 饮料 / 饮用 }   { 占（占有）/ 站（站立）}

字词运用

讨论

大家可以讨论一下，这件事情到底应该怎么办。

主张

眼看要来不及了，他主张马上就走。

我们大家都赞成你的主张。

享受

不爱劳动光爱享受可不好。

假日人们来到海边,享受阳光、沙滩和新鲜的空气。

效果

你的动机虽好,但是方法不当(dàng),效果大打折扣。

我吃过这个药,效果不错。

天天游泳,减肥效果明显。

根据课文回答问题

1. 墨子创立了什么学派?
2. 请解释墨子"兼相爱"的观点。
3. 墨子的"兼相爱"与孔子的"爱人"有什么不同?
4. 请解释墨子"交相利"的观点。

词语解释

不劳而获——自己不劳动而取得别人的劳动成果。

墨子简介

墨子名翟,战国时期鲁国人,墨家学派创始人,曾在宋国当过官。他主张勤劳、克苦、为他人,反对诸侯相互吞并的战争,提出"兼爱"、"非攻"等主张,著有《墨子》一书。

墨子救宋

公元前440年,楚国准备用鲁班制造的云梯攻打宋国。墨子听到消息后,一面派弟子三百余人赶往宋国,帮助宋国守城,一面亲自赶往楚国去说服楚王停止这场战争。墨子一路辛苦,走了十天十夜,终于来到楚国。

他见了楚王,说:"现在有一个人,他自己有漂亮的车子,还去偷邻居家破烂的车子;他自己有丝绸绣衣,还去偷邻居家破旧的衣衫;他自己有精美的肉食,还去偷邻居家粗糙的饭菜。这算是什么人呢?"楚王说:"这个人一定是犯了偷窃的毛病。"墨子接着说:"我听说您准备攻打宋国,与这个偷窃邻居的人有什么不同呢?如果攻打宋国,您必定失去了'义'而得不到宋。"墨子的话使楚王犹豫起来。

过了一会儿,楚王说:"鲁班已为我造好了攻城的云梯,我还是想攻打宋国。"于是墨子解下身上的皮带当做城池,用一些

小木板与鲁班"演练"了一场攻守战。鲁班用云梯攻城,墨子守城,最后,鲁班"战败"。鲁班说:"我还有办法,可是我不说。"墨子说:"我知道你的办法,我也不说。"他们的对话楚王没有听明白,便问道:"你们这是什么意思?"墨子说:"鲁班不过是要大王杀我。他以为杀了我,宋国就无法守城了。其实,我的三百多名弟子已经到宋国做好守城的准备了。您就是杀了我,楚国也打不了胜仗。"楚王听了以后,终于放弃了对宋国的战争。

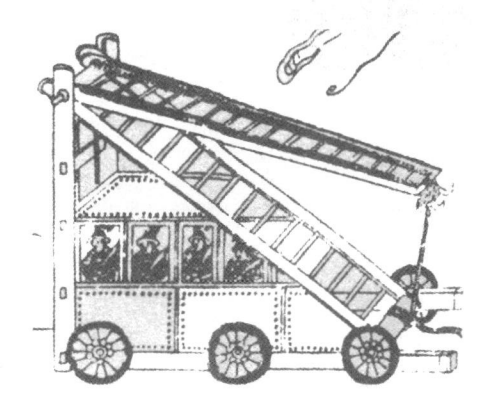

墨子救宋的故事,是墨家学派"兼爱"、"非攻",主张和平的体现。

生词

mò dí 墨翟	Mo Di (name)	pí dài 皮带	belt
zhū hóu 诸侯	duke or prince	yǎn liàn 演练	perform
tōu qiè 偷窃	steal	fàng qì 放弃	give up; quit
yóu yù 犹豫	hesitate	zhì zhǐ 制止	stop

Lesson Four

Thought of Mo Zi

Mo Zi (about 475 B.C.—396 B.C.), an important Chinese thinker and philosopher, established a new philosophy called Mohism. He, along with the majority of his students, often discussed the issue of labor and attached great emphasis on labor and fruit of labor since they are all handicraftsmen. In his opinion, man is different from other animals in that other animals have furs and feathers as clothes, claws and paws as shoes, grass and water as food and drinks, thus they may survive without labor; while man is different. Only by working can he be clothed and fed then survive. Therefore it is a must for everybody to work. Is it right for a person to steal fruits from others' orchard? The answer is absolutely not right, because he tried to get the fruit of others' labor without work. Man can only enjoy the fruit of labor by doing the work. It is immoral to gain without pains. Mo Zi's main thoughts are as follows:

First, "Universal Love": It means people should love each other. Mo Zi also thought that the best virtue is to love people, but his idea is different from "partiality of love" put forward by Confucius and Mencius. Confucius and Mencius held that people love their own parents first, then the others' parents; people's own immediate family members take precedence over the others' relatives; people love their parents more than the others' parents, love their own immediate families more than the others' relatives. This is called "partiality of love". But Mo Zi didn't think there should be any partiality in loving people. People should love the other's nation the same as their own nations, love the others' parents just as their own parents, and love the others just as themselves. Loving people should start with people themselves. People should love the others first, then they themselves will get the others' love; people should love the others' parents first, then the others will love their parents; people should love the others' nation first, then the others will love their nations. If people, families and nations love each other, there would be no fights and wars any more in the world.

Second, "Mutual Benefit": "Mutual Benefit" means getting benefit from each other. Mo Zi claimed that judging whether a person's behaviors are moral or not will depend on the results of actions as well as his motivation of actions. An action is considered moral only when it is motivated by loving people and bringing people actual benefits at the same time. Thus, "Universal Love" should reflect on "Mutual Benefit", i.e. getting benefits from each other. Mo Zi advocated that people should help each other: the strong help the weak, the rich help the poor, and the learned help the illiterate, so that the old people without family members and the orphans without parents could have means of livelihood, so that all the people could live a good life. It is immoral for the big, the strong and the rich to bully the small, the weak and the poor, no matter whether it is a nation or a person.

A Brief Introduction to Mo Zi

Mo Zi, whose given name is Di, was born in the state of Lu (or Song) during the Warring States Period. He was the founder of Mohism and had been an officer of Song state. He advocated hard work, self-restraint, altruism and condemned offensive wars between different states. He proclaimed "Universal Love", "Condemnation of War" etc. All of these ideas are recorded in his monograph titled *Mo Zi*

Mo Zi Saving the State of Song

In B. C.440, the state of Chu decided to attack the state of Song by using Lu Ban's Cloud-ladders. Hearing the news, Mo Zi immediately he sent about 300 disciples to the state of Song for protecting the city; simultaneously, he hurried to the state of Chu in person, trying to persuade the King of Chu to stop the war. It was a very tiring trip. It took him ten days and ten nights to walk to the state of Chu.

When Mo Zi met the King of Chu, he asked him, "there was such a person: he had a very beautiful carriage, but he still stole his neighbor's damaged cart; he had splendid silk clothes, but he still stole his neighbor's shabby clothes; he had very good food, but he still stole his neighbor's crude food. So could you please tell me what kind of person he is?" The King of Chu answered: "he must have got into the habit of stealing." Then Mo Zi continued, "I heard that you were going to attack the state of Song, is it the same case with this? If you attack the state of Song, you are sure to lose the virtue of 'righteousness' thus won't get the state of Song." These words set the King of Chu into hesitation.

After a while, the King of Chu said, "Since Lu Ban had already made the Cloud-ladders, I still wanted to use it to attack Song." Hearing this, Mo Zi untied the belt from his body, laid out an imagined city with it, and made a "demonstration" of attack and defense with Lu Ban by some small boards. Lu Ban attacked the city by Cloud-ladders and Mo Zi tried his best to defend the city. At last, it ended up with Lu Ban's "being defeated". Then Lu Ban said: "I have another way, but I will not tell you." Mo Zi replied, "I know your way and I won't tell either." Confused by such dialogue, the King of Chu could not help asking them "what do you mean?" Mo Zi explained, "Lu Ban means to ask Your Majesty to kill me, so that the state of Song could not defend its city any more. In fact, more than 300 of my disciples have already arrived there and are ready for defense. Even if you killed me, Chu couldn't win." Hearing this, the King of Chu finally gave up the war to the state of Song.

The story of Mo Zi saving the state of Song mainly represents Mohism's "Universal Love", "Condemnation of War" and advocating peaceful settlement of disputes.

第五课

老子的思想

老子（约前606—前586）是中国最重要的思想家、哲学家之一，他的思想充分体现了中国人的智慧，对东方国家甚至全世界都有很大的影响。他创立了道家学派。

一、"反者道之动"。老子的思想是围绕着他对"道"的理解展开的。"道"就是道路，就是天地万物都要走过的道路。用哲学语言讲，"道"就是规律、法则。它的主要内

老子骑牛图　（明）张　路

容是"反者道之动"，意思是说，任何事物都会走向自己的反面。老子认为，世界上的事物都有自己的对立面，都有一种东西和自己相反，比如大与小、多与少、高与低、前与后、长与短、生与死、成功与失败等等。每一种事物都以自己的对立面为前提，比如没有高就没有低，没有恶就

没有善，没有假就没有真，没有丑就没有美。每一种事物发展到了顶点就会走向自己的反面，比如太阳升到了最高点就会慢慢落下去，天气到了最冷的时候就会逐渐变暖，人生长到了顶点就会一天天走向死亡。这条道路是每一个人、每一个事物都要走的，这是天地万物发展变化的规律。

二、"柔弱胜刚强"。因为事物都会走向自己的反面，所以老子认为弱小的事物最有生命力，要比强大的事物更有力量，弱小的事物能够战胜强大的事物。他举例说："世界上的事物没有比水更柔弱的了，可是它最能攻破坚硬的东西。"大家都知道，水虽然很柔软，但没有任何东西能打破它，用刀子砍不断它，用铁锤砸不烂它。可是水却能冲坏坚硬的东西。屋檐上的雨水往下滴，时间长了能把下面的石头打出一个洞来。这就叫做"柔弱胜刚强"。无论是一个人还是一个国家，要想长期生存下去，就要保持柔弱的状态。老子说："人活着的时候总是柔软的，死后就变得坚硬了。花草树木活着的时候总是柔软的，死后就变得又干又硬了。"同样的道理，我们要想打败自己的敌人，就要先让它强大起来；我们要想夺取敌人的东西，就要先给它一些东西。任何东西都不会长久不变的，一旦它强大了，也就会逐渐衰落了。

三、"无为而无不为"。"道"不是任何一种具体的事物，可是一切事物都是从"道"中走出来的，一切事物都要按照"道"的规定生存和发展。作为一个国家的领导人，也要像"道"一样"无为"。"无为"就是不做任何具体的事情，不管任何一个具体的部门。如果你去管理外交部，就无法管理内务部；如果你带领军队去打仗，就无法去组织社会生产。一个国家的最高领导人只有不去做任何具体的事情，不去管理任何具体的部门，才能做好所有的事情，管理好所有的部门。这就叫做"无为而无不为"。

生词

chōng fèn 充分	full; abundant	wū yán 屋檐	eaves
wéi rào 围绕	surround; focus	gāng qiáng 刚强	firm; staunch
lǐ jiě 理解	understand; comprehend	bǎo chí 保持	keep; maintain
fǎ zé 法则	rule; law	duó qǔ 夺取	capture; occupy
duì lì miàn 对立面	opposite; antithesis	yí dàn 一旦	once; in case
qián tí 前提	premise	jù tǐ 具体	specific; particular
chǒu 丑	ugliness	wài jiāo 外交	diplomacy; foreign affairs
jiān yìng 坚硬	hard	nèi wù 内务	domestic affairs
róu ruǎn 柔软	soft		

听写

充分　外交　具体　无论　刚强　理解　坚硬

丑　法则　*围绕　柔弱

比一比

具 { 具体 / 具有 / 工具 }　　持 { 保持 / 持久 / 主持 }　　则 { 法则 / 原则 }　　发 { 发明 / 发现 }

柔 { 柔软 / 柔弱 }　　强 { 刚强 / 强壮 }　　提 { 前提 / 提高 }　　顶 { 顶点 / 顶天立地 }

字词运用

充分

老子的思想充分体现了中国人的智慧。

离考试还有三个星期,我有充分的时间复习功课。

一旦

一旦学生迷上电子游戏，他的学习就会常常受到影响。

一旦下雪，上山的路就不通了。

一旦学会开车，我就自由了。

保持

同学们要注意保持教室的清洁卫生。

老师说："上课要保持安静。"

中国乒乓球队男子单打，连续六年保持世界冠军。

近义词

规律——法则　　　　　　无论——不论

反义词

柔弱——刚强　　　　　　正面——反面

柔软——坚硬　　　　　　美——丑

根据课文回答问题

1. 老子是什么时期的人，他创立了什么学派？

2. 老子认为："世界上的事物都有自己的对立面，都有一种东西和自己相反。"你的看法呢？

3. 请解释下列老子的观点："反者道之动"、"柔弱胜刚强"、"无为而无不为"。

阅读

老子简介

老子，春秋时期大哲学家，道家学派的创始人。他出生在楚国，姓李，名耳，字伯阳，又称老聃。老子从小爱读书，他广泛阅读了各种书籍。二十多岁时，在东周都城洛阳当上了管理国家图书的官，后来逐渐成为知名的大学问家，著有《道德经》一书。当时常有人向他请教问题，相传孔子曾向他问礼。

孔子问"礼"

孔子曾经专门到洛阳向老子请教"礼"的知识。孔子引用了许多古代圣贤关于礼制的话向老子请教。老子淡淡一笑，对孔子说："孔丘啊，你提到的这些古代圣贤都已经死去很久了，恐怕埋在地下的骨头都腐烂了吧，就剩下这些话还流传于世。所以你不必去模仿他们，用这些话约束自己的言行。君子应该有适应社会的能力，碰到机会就轰轰烈烈地干一番事业；没有机会就远离政治，无拘无束地生活。你觉得是不是这个道理？"孔子听了很受启发。

关于老子的《道德经》

老子一直住在洛阳，周景王死后，爆发了长达五年的内战。败兵逃走时，带走了图书馆许多珍贵的书籍，这让老子很难过。他左思右想，决定去战乱极少的秦国安度晚年。

老子骑着青牛上路了。没走几日，便来到了函谷关口，过了函谷关就进入秦国了。正在这时，守关的官员尹喜迎出来恭恭敬敬地向老子行礼说："先生经过这里，没能远迎，希望您别见怪。先生学问广博，见识深远，既然路过这里，请您小住几日，将您的见解写成一部书，一可让我拜读，二可让天下百姓受到您的教诲，请您不要推辞！"

老子被尹喜的真挚所感动，便住下来，把自己关于道、德、无为而治、以弱胜强以及对宇宙、人生、社会等方面的见解，全部融于一书之中，写成一部五千余字的《道德经》。这部书最核心的内容是"道"，老子认为"道"是宇宙的本源，世界上万事万物的形成和发展，都由"道"转化和生成，它像天地一样永不停息地运动，它的规律就是自然的规律、社会的规律。

成书以后，老子继续西行，此后他的下落就没有人知道了。

生词

lǎo dān 老聃	Lao Dan (a form of address for Lao Zi)	yǐn 尹	Yin (surname)
mó fǎng 模仿	emulate; imitate	jiàn guài 见怪	mind; take offense
jūn zǐ 君子	a man of noble character	guǎng bó 广博	learned
hōng hōng liè liè 轰轰烈烈	vigorous	jiàn jiě 见解	view; opinion
wú jū wú shù 无拘无束	unrestrained	jiào huì 教诲	instructions; teachings
qǐ fā 启发	enlighten	zhēn zhì 真挚	sincere
ān dù wǎn nián 安度晚年	enjoy the later life	róng yú ... zhī zhōng 融于……之中	merge into
hán gǔ guān 函谷关	Han Gu Pass	hé xīn 核心	core; kernel
		xià luò 下落	where abouts

 English Translation

Lesson Five

Thought of Lao Zi

Lao Zi (about 606 B.C.—586 B. C.) was one of the most important Chinese thinkers and philosophers. His thought fully represents the wisdom of Chinese people and has exerted great influence on the whole world as well as the oriental countries. The philosophy he established is called Taoism or Tao Jia. His main thoughts are as follows:

First, "Cycling is the movement of the *Tao*": Centered on the interpretation of "*Tao*", thought of Lao Zi pointed out that "*Tao*" is the way, in which everything has to pass. In philosophical terms, "*Tao*" means laws and rules. Its main content is "Cycling is the movement of the *Tao*", which means that everything will be destined to be its opposites. Lao Zi held that everything in the world has its own opposites and there should exist something that is opposite to it, such as big and small, many and few, high and low, front and back, long and short, life and death, success and failure. Everything exists with its opposites as the premise. For instance, if there is no "high", then there is no "low"; no evil, no good; no false, no truth; no ugliness, no beauty. Everything will go downwards when reaching its climax, like the sun going set when rising at the highest, weather becoming warmer when it be coldest and men going on the way to death when getting very old. This is the way that everybody and everything should pass. This is the law by which everything in the world develops.

Second, "The soft conquers the hard; and the weak the strong." Since things will inevitably move towards their opposites, Lao Zi held that weak and soft things are usually more powerful and vigorous than strong and hard things, thus the former can beat the latter. He took water as an example, "Nothing in the world is suppler than water, yet nothing is more powerful than water in attacking the hard and strong." As we all know, water is very soft, but nothing can break it either by the knife or the hammer. Conversely, water can damage something hard. Water can dig a hole in the stone under the eaves if it keeps dripping from the eaves onto the stone for a long time. This is the case of that "the weak conquers the strong". Be it a person or a nation, if it hopes to be long-lasting, it should remain soft and weak. As Lao Zi once said, "When alive, a man's body is supple; when dead, it becomes hard. When alive, grass and trees are supple; when dead, they become dry and stiff." The same truth is also applicable to fighting with the enemy. If we want to defeat the enemies, we must let them be stronger first; if we want to capture something from the enemies, we must give some benefits to them first. Everything cannot remain unchangeable and it will decline gradually once it becomes extremely strong.

Third, "When reaching the state of inaction, one can succeed in everything." "*Tao*" is not something specific, yet everything specific originates from it, lives and grows by it. Therefore, a nation's leaders should behave inactively like the way *Tao* does. "Inaction" means doing nothing specific, managing no specific branch. If you are in charge of the Ministry of Foreign Affairs, you cannot manage the Department of Domestic Affairs; if you are leading a troop for fighting in the battlefield, then you cannot organize the social production. Thus, the supreme leader of a nation can manage everything and all branches well only if he does not do anything specific or regulate any specific branch. This is the true sense of what we say "When reaching the state of inaction, one can succeed in everything".

A Brief Introduction to Lao Zi

Lao Zi was a great philosopher during the Spring and Autumn Period as well as the founder of Taoism. He was born in the state of Chu, whose sir name is Li, given name Er, appellation Boyang, and also called as "Lao Dan". Lao Zi loved reading since childhood and had read many kinds of books. In his twenties, he served as an officer taking care of the state's books in Luoyang, the capital of Eastern Zhou Dynasty. Later on, he became a well-known man of great learning and wrote a book titled *Tao Teh Ching*. He was so learned that many people came to inquire of him about puzzles. One legend is that Confucius once inquired of him about the rites.

Confucius Inquiry about "Rites"

It was said that Confucius once made a special trip to Luoyang and inquired of Lao Zi about "rites" by quoting a lot of remarks of those ancient great men. Smiling slightly, Lao Zi made an answer to Confucius, "Kong Qiu, those great ancient men you mentioned had been dead for a long time and maybe their bones had been decayed. Only those words had been handed down to this very day. In my opinion, it is not necessary for you to emulate them and use their words to conduct your behaviors. A man of noble character is supposed to adjust himself to the world. As luck would have it, you may make a great success in your career; if there is no good chance, you may live a carefree life by not interfering with politics. Do you think my words make sense?" Confucius was greatly enlightened by such words.

About Lao Zi's *Tao Teh Ching*

Lao Zi had been living in Luoyang, where there broke out a five-year-long civil war after the death of King Jing of Zhou Dynasty. The defeated army took away a lot of valuable books in their retreat, which made Lao Zi very sad. After deliberate consideration, he decided to enjoy his later life in the state of Qin where there were fewer wars.

Lao Zi went on his way by riding a bull. Several days later, he came to Han Gu Pass, across which he may enter the state of Qin. Just at this moment, the officer named Yin Xi, who was defending the gate, came out to salute to Lao Zi, saying "I felt so sorry that I didn't go to welcome you before you came and please forgive me for this misconduct. You are known to be learned and far-sighted. Why not live here for some days to write a book of your opinions so that I can read it and the ordinary people can get benefited? Please do not turn me down."

Moved by Yin Xi's sincerity, Lao Zi began to settle himself down there and integrated all opinions about *Tao*, virtues, non-action policy, the weak-conquering-the strong and other viewpoints about the universe, life and society into one book entitled *Tao Teh Ching* in about five thousand Chinese characters. The core of this book is "*Tao*", which is, in Lao Zi's opinion, the origin of the universe. He thought the growth and development of everything in the world is generated and transformed by "*Tao*", which keeps moving all the time like heaven and earth. Its law is the law of nature, the law of society.

After the book was finished, Lao Zi went continuously westward, but nobody knew where he had gone to.

第六课

庄子的思想

庄子（约前369—前286）是中国重要的思想家、哲学家，道家学派的主要代表人物之一。他的思想在中国思想史、哲学史、文学史上有很高的地位。

庄子像

一、"道"。庄子的思想也是围绕着"道"展开的，不过他对"道"的理解与老子有所不同。老子所说的"道"主要是指"反者道之动"，而庄子说的"道"主要有两个方面：一个方面是指整个宇宙，一切事物都包括在其中；另一个方面是指宇宙的运动变化，天地万物不停的运动变化就是"道"。庄子的"道"有两个特征：其一，"道"是天地万物的全体而不是任何一种具体的事物，任何一种具体的事物都是有限的，而"道"是无限的，所以"道"是"无"而不是"有"；其二，"道"是自然而

然地存在,自然而然地运动变化,一切事物自己的存在和变化都是"道"。

二、自然。庄子说的自然不是自然界,而是自然而然。比如刮风下雨是自然,人饿了吃饭、渴了喝水也是自然,一切非人为的存在和变化都是自然。庄子认为,世界上一切事物都是自然而然地存在着,自然而然地变化着。任何事物都有自己的本性,都有自己的生存方式,都有自己的功用。比如马这种动物,蹄子可以踏霜雪,皮毛可以御风寒,吃草喝水,相互戏耍,这是马的自然,它们喜欢这样生活。人们给马带上了马鞍,让它拉车,骑上它赛跑,训练它,用皮鞭打它,这就破坏了马的自然。世界上的事物都是这样,鹤的腿很长,如果把它的腿截短了,它就不能生活了。鸡的腿很短,如果把它的腿加长了,它就会因为无法吃到地上的食物而饿死。因此人应该尊重自然、顺应自然,而不要按照自己的愿望去改变自然、破坏自然、打扰自然。只有这样,世界才能更好地存在,人类才能更好地生存。

三、自由。庄子喜欢讲故事,他说:"北海里有一条大鱼,鱼的身体有几千里长。大鱼变成了一只鸟,鸟的脊背有几千里宽。大鸟要飞到南海去。它一起飞,海水被击起

了三千里高的大浪。它乘着水和空气的力量飞到九万里的高空,翅膀像乌云那样遮住天日,一直飞了六个月才飞到南海。大鸟的飞行多么壮观、多么自由啊!"可是,庄子认为这还不是真正的自由,它还需要凭借空气和水的力量,真正的自由是无条件的。什么样的自由是无条件的呢?庄子说"乘天地之正,而御六气之变,以游无穷者"是不需要条件的。也就是说,随着自然的变化而变化,随着自然的运动而运动才是无条件的自由,才是真正的自由。这样的人需要忘掉自己的存在,把自己融入到自然的变化中去。

王金泰 画

生词

dài biǎo 代表	represent		xùn liàn 训练	train; drill
dì wèi 地位	position; status		jié duǎn 截短	cut short
zhěng gè 整个	whole; entire		shùn yìng 顺应	comply with; conform to
yí qiè 一切	all; everything		dǎ rǎo 打扰	disturb; trouble
tè zhēng 特征	features; characteristic		jǐ bèi 脊背	back
cún zài 存在	existence		píng jiè 凭借	rely on; depend on
gōng yòng 功用	function; use		tiáo jiàn 条件	condition
shuāng 霜	frost and snow		róng rù 融入	merge
xì shuǎ 戏耍	play with			

听写

代表　整个　训练　一切　地位　打扰　条件　戏耍

脊背　特征　*霜　融入

比一比

表 { 代表 / 钟表 }　　功 { 功能 / 功夫 }　　整 { 整个 / 整齐 }

顺 { 顺应 / 顺利 }　　特 { 特征 / 特别 }　　位 { 地位 / 位置 }

字词运用

一切

我们已经做好了一切准备，就等着出发了。

你放心走吧，这里一切都有人照管。

我在学校一切都好，请妈妈放心。

条件

想跟我去游泳有一个条件，要做完作业。

这里的居住条件很好，又安全，又方便。

代表

吴霜代表我们班参加演讲比赛。

近义词

整个——全部　　　　一切——所有　　　　凭借——依靠

反义词

有限——无限

根据课文回答问题

1. 庄子是什么时期的人，是什么学派的代表人物？

2. 什么是庄子讲的"道"？他对"道"的理解与老子有什么不同？

3. 庄子认为："人应该尊重自然、顺应自然，而不应该按照自己的愿望去改变自然、破坏自然、打扰自然。这样，世界才能更好地存在，人类才能更好地存在。"你的看法如何？

中国古代哲学

> 阅读

庄子简介

庄子名周，宋国（今河南商丘）人，战国时期的哲学家、文学家，道家学派的代表人物之一。庄子的文章华丽而浪漫，善于运用打比方和讲故事的方法阐述道理，表达观点。

庄子与楚王

楚威王听说庄子很有才能，派人带着礼物去请他到楚国当宰

王金泰　画

相。使者见到庄子，恭恭敬敬地说："我们大王听说先生贤明能干，派我来请先生当楚国的宰相。"庄子微微一笑，说："宰相是个不小的官位，大王给的金钱也不少。你有没有见过太庙里当祭品的牛？每天喂它们大豆、青草，养得它们又肥又壮，小猪羡慕它们有这么好的运气。但是后来，这些牛都会被披上彩色的绸子，拉到太庙里当祭品宰杀了。恐怕这时候它们要羡慕小猪自由自在的生活了。我宁愿像小猪那样过贫寒的自由生活，也不愿做官受约束，最后还可能像那些牛一样逃不过被杀的命运。"使者只好回到楚国去了。

生词

chǎn shù 阐述	expound; elabrate		pī 披	drape over
dí què 的确	indeed; really		chóu zi 绸子	silk fabric
jì pǐn 祭品	sacrifices		nìng yuàn 宁愿	would rather
xiàn mù 羡慕	admire		táo bu guò 逃不过	unable to escape

问题

庄子为什么不愿意做楚国的宰相？

 *English Translation*

Lesson Six

Thought of Zhuang Zi

Zhuang Zi (about 369 B.C.—286 B.C.) was an important Chinese thinker and philosopher as well as one of the main representatives of Taoists. His thought ranks high in the Chinese history of thought, philosophy and literature. The essence of his thought is as follows:

First, "*Tao*": Thought of Zhuang Zi is also centered on "*Tao*", but which is different from what Lao Zi advocated, "Cycling is the movement of the *Tao*". "*Tao*" by Zhuang Zi refers to two aspects: one is the universe, in which everything has been included; another is the movement of the universe. The movement and changes of everything in the world constitutes "*Tao*". In Zhuang Zi's opinion, there are two characteristics of "*Tao*": first, "*Tao*" is the whole of everything rather than anything specific because any specific thing is limited while "*Tao*" is infinitive, implying "Nothingness" instead of "Being"; second, "*Tao*" is the natural existence and natural movement. The existence and change of everything makes what is "*Tao*".

Second, Naturalness: Here it does not refer to the Nature, but naturalness. For example, it is natural to have wind and rains; it is natural for people to eat when hungry, to drink when thirsty. All non-man-made existences and changes are naturalness. Zhuang Zi held that everything in the world exists naturally and changes in a natural way. Everything has its own nature, its own way of living and its own function. Take horses as an example. Their natural way of living is like this: their hoofs can tread frost and snow and their fur can defend the cold. They are grazing, drinking and playing with each other as they like. But if people put saddles on the horse, make it drive the carts, ride it for race, train it, or whip it, that's the destruction of the naturalness of horses. It is true with all the other existences. A crane with long legs cannot live if we cut its legs shorter; a rooster with short legs will die of hunger because of being unable to eat the food on the ground, if we make its legs longer. Therefore, people should respect the Nature and adapt themselves to the Nature rather than change, destruct or interfere with the Nature at their own will. Only in this way can the world exist in a better way and human beings live a better life.

Third, Freedom: Zhuang Zi loved telling stories, and illustrated it in a story like this: "In the North Sea, there was once a big fish with a body of a few thousand *li* long. Later on, this big fish transformed into a bird with a back of a few thousand *li* wide. It intended to fly to the South Sea. When it departed to fly toward the sky, the water was splashed into a height of three thousand *li*. With the support of water and air, it flew into a height of 90,000 *li*, its wings spreading like clouds covering the sun. It kept flying for six months until it arrived at the South Sea. How splendidly and how freely it flew!" However, Zhuang Zi had a different thought that this was not the true freedom since it still needs the support of air and water. In his opinion, true freedom was unconditional. What kind of freedom is unconditional? Zhuang Zi pointed out

that someone who "chariots on the normality of the universe, rides on the transformations of the six elements, and thus makes an excursion into infinite", enjoys unconditional freedom. That is to say, the true freedom, the unconditional freedom is the freedom which can change and move with the Nature. Such freedom can be achieved only when man forgets his own existence and merges himself into the natural changes.

A Brief Introduction to Zhuang Zi

Zhuang Zi, really named Zhuang Zhou, was born in the state of Song (in the present Shangqiu of Henan Province). He was a philosopher and man of letters during the Warring States Period, also one of the main representatives of Taoist. He was good at expressing his thought by means of metaphors and similes and making up stories in romantic and flowery language.

The Story of Zhuang Zi and the King of Chu

Once upon a time, hearing that Zhuang Zi was very capable, the King of Chu (Wei Wang) sent ambassadors to invite him to be the prime minister of Chu with generous gifts. Seeing Zhuang Zi, the ambassador said very respectfully, "our King highly appreciated your high abilities and wisdom, so he sent me to invite you to be the prime minister of Chu." Hearing this, Zhuang Zi replied with a smile, saying that "being a prime minister is a high official rank, and the money provided by the King is pretty much as well. Have you ever seen the cows that are offered as sacrifices in the Imperial Ancestral Temple? They are fed on beans and green grass, growing very fat and strong, which is highly admired by piglets. But finallyall these cows will be dressed in colorful silks and sent to be killed as sacrifices. At that time, maybe it is cows' turn to admire the free life of piglets. I would rather live a poor but very free life like piglets, than be an official restrained by the rules and probably unable to escape from being killed like those cows in the end." The ambassador had to go back to the state of Chu.

第七课

孙子的思想

孙子像

孙子（孔子同时代人，生卒年月不详）是中国古代伟大的军事家。他写过一部书，叫做《孙子兵法》，系统地论述了战争中的各种问题，在世界上有很大影响。直到现在，还有许多政治家、军事家、实业家学习它。

一、敌我。任何战争都分为敌方和我方。在战争开始之前，最重要的工作就是要清楚地了解敌我双方的情况，包括：哪一方是正义的，哪一方是非正义的；哪一方的统帅更会打仗；哪一方的地形更有利；哪一方的战士更有训练；哪一方的纪律更严明。把这些情况都了解清楚了，也就知道谁胜谁败了。孙子说："知己知彼，百战不殆。"了解自己又了解敌人，才能制定正确的作战方案，这样才会百战百胜。

二、攻守。孙子说："善攻者敌不知其所守，善守者敌不知其所攻。"战争总是有攻有守，进攻时要攻其不备，出其不意，要在敌人想不到的时间、想不到的地点发起进攻，要向敌人防守最薄弱地方或者是敌人的要害发起进攻，让敌人跑不掉。防守时要使敌人不知道从哪里进攻，不知道你的薄弱处在哪里、你的要害在哪里，让敌人不敢追赶。三国时诸葛亮带领蜀军和魏军打仗，撤退时一路走一路让士兵们多修灶。魏军追了几天，看见蜀军用来做饭的灶一天比一天多，以为蜀军一路上到处都有伏兵，于是就不敢再追了。这在中国兵法上叫做"增灶法"。孙膑（bìn）（孙子的后代）打仗也用过这个方法，不过他用的不是"增灶法"而是"减灶法"。孙膑带领军队撤退，一路走一路让士兵们少修灶。敌人看见他们用来做饭的灶一天比一天少，以为他的士兵们每天都有不少人逃跑，于是便大胆地追了上去，结果中了孙膑的埋伏，被孙膑消灭了。

三、生死。孙子说："死地则战。"意思是说，在战争中，双方都会努力消灭敌人，保存自己。但是，有时候为了生存，必须先把自己置于死地。秦末战争中，韩信领兵攻打赵国。赵国的城市背后是高山，前面是大河，地形对韩信的军队非常不利。韩信又是新提拔的将领，威望不高。

在这种情况下,韩信带领军队坐船渡过大河以后就把船烧掉了。他指挥士兵们开始进攻,敌人反攻过来,他的士兵掉头就跑。士兵们跑到河边时,韩信高喊:"士兵们,我们已经无路可逃了,只有打败敌人,我们才能生存!"于是士兵们各个奋勇杀敌,打败了赵国。这在中国兵法上叫做"置之死地而后生"。

生 词

zú 卒	die	yào hài 要害	a place of strategic importance
lùn shù 论述	expound	shǔ 蜀	Shu (a kingdom of the three kingdoms)
shí yè 实业	industry; practice	chè tuì 撤退	retreat
tǒng shuài 统帅	commander	zào 灶	kitchen range
jì lǜ 纪律	discipline	bǎo cún 保存	save
yán míng 严明	strict and impartial	tí bá 提拔	promote
dài 殆	dangerous	wēi wàng 威望	prestige
zuò zhàn 作战	fight	dù 渡	cross
fāng àn 方案	plan	zhǐ huī 指挥	command; conduct
fáng shǒu 防守	defend	fèn yǒng 奋勇	courageously; bravely

听写

论述　保存　统帅　指挥　防守　严明　作战　渡

奋勇　纪律　*撤退　威望

比一比

存 { 保存 / 生存　　严 { 严明 / 严肃　　帅 { 统帅 / 帅哥　　挥 { 指挥 / 发挥

练 { 训练 / 练习　　方 { 方案 / 方面　　律 { 纪律 / 格律　　{ 渡（渡河）/ 度（温度）

字词运用

保存

这件东西很重要，你一定要把它保存好。

提拔

他是新提拔的军官。

这位新提拔的经理只有27岁。

威望

韩信是新提拔的将军,威望不高。

林肯是美国最有威望的总统之一。

要害

解决问题要抓住要害。

近义词

卒——死　　　　　　作战——打仗

根据课文回答问题

1. 《孙子兵法》一书是谁写的?

2. 请解释《孙子兵法》中的:"知己知彼,百战不殆"。

3. 选做题:你怎么理解"攻其不备,出其不意"?能不能举例说明?

孙子简介

孙子名武，齐国人，春秋时期的军事家。他写的《孙子兵法》是中国古代著名的兵书，也是世界上现存最早的军事著作。《孙子兵法》分为13篇，共6,000多字，在中国军事史上占有重要地位，在世界军事史上也享有极高声誉，已被翻译成英文、法文等多种文字。

孙武演兵

孙武精通兵法，一次去求见吴王阖闾。吴王说："你写的《孙子兵法》我看过了，写得非常好。你能当场为我表演一下吗？"孙武说："可以。"吴王问："可以用妇女操练演示吗？"孙武说："可以。"于是吴王从宫中挑选了一百八十名美女供孙武演练。孙武把她们分成两队，让吴王的两个妃子当队长，让宫女们拿着长矛站好。孙武把号令讲了几遍，问："听

孙子演兵图

明白了吗？"宫女们齐声答应："明白。"说完，孙武击鼓发出命令，可宫女们全都站在原地嬉笑，没有人听从他的命令。孙武说："这一次没做好，是我没把军法号令讲清楚，这是我做将领的过错。"于是，他把规定又讲了几遍，然后再次击鼓下令，宫女们仍然嬉笑不动。孙武严肃地说："号令讲得不明白，军法讲得不清楚，是将领的错；如果这些都讲清楚了，士兵们还不按规定做，那就是队长的过错了。"说着就要将左右两队的队长斩首。吴王急了，连忙对孙武说："我已经知道您善于用兵了。这两个女子，您就给我留下来吧！"孙武说："我已经接受命令当您的将军，将军在军队里可以不接受君王的命令。"说完，硬是把两个妃子斩了。大家见孙武军纪这么严明，再也不敢胡闹了。

后来，吴王阖闾任命孙武为吴国的大将。他率(shuài)军打败了强大的楚国，使吴王阖闾成为一代霸主。

生词

shēng yù 声誉	reputation; fame	jiàng lǐng 将领	general; military commander
hé lǘ 阖闾	He Lü (name)	yán sù 严肃	serious; grave
yǎn shì 演示	demonstrate	zhǎn shǒu 斩首	behead; cut one's head
fēi zi 妃子	concubine	hú nào 胡闹	play the fool; make trouble
xī xiào 嬉笑	play and laugh	bà zhǔ 霸主	*powerful chief of feudal lords princes*

Lesson Seven
Thought of Sun Zi

Sun Zi (the contemporary of Confucius, his date of birth and death unknown), a great ancient military strategist in China, had written a book entitled *The Art of War*, which elaborated systematically different issues in the war and exerted such great influence on the world that so many politicians, strategists and industrialists are still studying it. The main content of the book focuses on the following three aspects:

First, Enemy and ourselves: Any war is conducted between the enemy and our forces, so the most important step before the battle is to get to know the situations of the enemy and ourselves, such as: which side is righteous, and which side is unrighteous; whose general is better at commanding; which side is located in a better geographical condition; whose soldiers are better trained; whose disciplines are more strict. A clear understanding of all these can indicate who is going to win, just as Sun Zi had put it, "Know the enemy and ourselves, then it is sure to win all the wars and never fail". It implies that only after you get to know both the enemy and yourself can you make appropriate military plans, which can lead to the final win.

Second, Attack and defense: Sun Zi once said, "The general is skillful in attack whose opponent does not know what to defend; and he is skillful in defense whose opponent does not know what to attack". It means any war will involve attack and defense, so people need to attack the enemies when the enemies are not getting prepared or just attack them out of their expectations, to attack them in unexpected time and place, to attack the enemies' weakest points or the most crucial places, so that the enemies could not escape. When in defense, you need make the enemies not know where to attack, not know your weak points and your crucial places, making enemies dare not chase if your troop retreat. Here are two good examples to illustrate this tactic. During the period of Three Kingdoms, Zhuge Liang, when leading Shu troop to fight against Wei troop, asked his soldiers to build stoves one after another on the way of retreat. Running after them for several days, Wei troop came to find the cooking stoves increasing in numbers and suspected there must be some soldiers in ambush, so they gave up chasing Shu troop. Such tactic is called "the strategy of building more stoves". Another case is about Sun Bin (the descendent of Sun Zi), who employed the same strategy in opposite way named "the strategy of building fewer stoves". When retreating, Sun Bin ordered his soldiers to build fewer stoves on the way. Then when the enemies found the number of cooking stoves became less, and thought there must be some soldiers running away from the troops every day, so they chased with great courage and turned out to be attacked by Sun Bin's ambush, totally defeated.

Third, Life and death: Sun Zi once said, "Place your army in deadly peril, and it will survive." It implies that both sides will try its best to kill the enemy and save itself in any war. But sometimes people need to put themselves in a desperate situation for the sake of survival. In a battle taking place at the end of Qin Dynasty, Han Xin commanded soldiers to attack the state of Zhao. The battlefield was located in an unfavorable geographic condition, with big rivers ahead and high mountains in the back. Han Xin, a newly promoted commander, was not so prestigious. Considering such conditions, Han Xin got the ship burned as soon as the soldiers crossed the river. When the battle began, Han Xin directed the soldiers to fight, but the soldiers tried to run away at the enemies' attack. When the soldiers ran to the riverside, Han Xin shouted, "Dear soldiers, we had no way out. Only defeating the enemies can we survive." Without any choice, the soldiers had to fight bravely and defeated the state of Zhao.

In Chinese military art, such strategy is called "Place your army in deadly peril and it will survive".

A Brief Introduction to Sun Zi

Sun Zi, named Sun Wu, was a citizen of the State of Qi in the Spring and Autumn Period. His book entitled *The Art of war* is considered as the earliest existing military book in the world as well as a famous Chinese classic on military art in ancient China. This book was written in thirteen chapters in more than 6,000 words. Now it occupies an important status in Chinese military history and also enjoys a high popularity in the world military history. It has already been translated into other foreign languages such as English and French.

Sun Wu Demonstrating the Military Art

Sun Wu was a good master of military arts. Once he went to visit He Lv, the King of Wu. The king said, "I have read your book *The Art of War* and it was pretty well written. Can you demonstrate it on the spot for me?" "Sure," replied Sun Wu. "Can the women act as the soldiers of performance?" The King asked. "Yes," Sun Wu agreed.

Then the King of Wu chose 180 beauties from the palace for Sun Wu to demonstrate military art. First, Sun Wu divided them into two groups, assigning the king's two favorite concubines to be the group leaders and others to stand straight with long shears. Then Sun Wu repeated the orders for several times, and then asked them, "Are you all clear?" "Yes," all the women answered in chorus. After that, Sun Wu beat the drum to give orders, but none of them obeyed his orders, standing at the original place to laugh and play casually. Seeing this, Sun Wu said, "We didn't do it well this time because I didn't explain the military orders clearly and this is my fault as a commander." So he repeated the rules several times more, then beat the drum to give orders again, but all the women still remained there laughing and playing casually, which angered Su Wu so much that he said seriously, "if the directions are not clear and the military orders are not explicit, it is the commander's fault; but if all of these are clearly explained while the soldiers refuse to obey the rules, then it is the group leaders' fault." When finishing these words, Sun Wu ordered to kill the two leaders. The King was shocked and hurried to persuade Sun Wu, "I got to know that you are very good at commanding soldiers and please save these two ladies for me." But Su Wu answered, "I have accepted your order to be your commander. While in the army, a commander may have the right not to obey the King's order." Finishing the remarks, he kept his order and killed the King's two favorite concubines. Witnessing that Sun Wu was so strict in military disciplines, nobody dared do at her own will any more.

Later on, He Lv, the King of Wu appointed Sun Wu the command-in-chief of Wu. He led the armies to defeat the powerful state of Chu, making He Lv the most powerful overlord of that time.

第八课

《易经》的思想

（选读课）

《易经》是儒家的主要经典之一。"易"有三层意思。第一层意思是变化，这部书是讲变化的。第二层意思是简明，它用符号表示不同的事物和事物的变化。它用的符号只有两个，一个是"—"，叫做"阳"，代表天、太阳、光明、刚强、积极、运动、温暖的力量；一个是"--"，叫做"阴"，代表地、月亮、黑暗、柔弱、消极、静止、寒冷的力量。把这

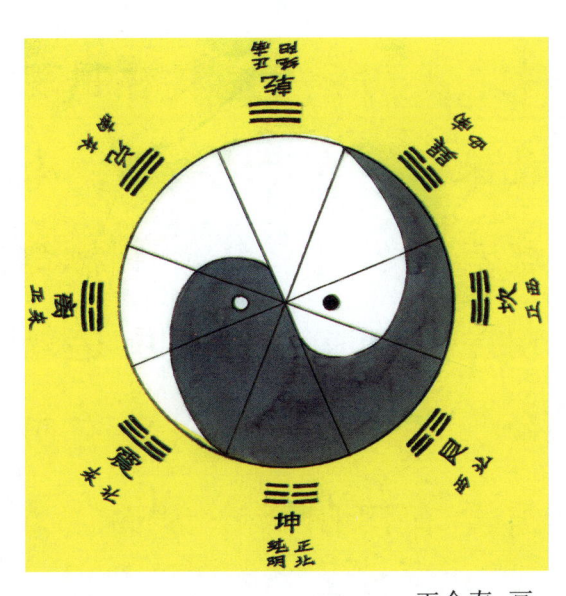

王金泰 画

两个符号三个一组排列起来可以得到八组符号，这八组符号叫做"八卦"，它们是：乾(qián)、坤(kūn)、坎(kǎn)、离、艮(gèn)、兑(duì)、巽(xùn)、震，分别代表天、地、水、火、山、泽、风、雷八种事物。再把这八组符号两个一组排列起来又可以得到六十四组符号，叫做"六十四卦"，代表事物之间的不同关系和变化。第三

层意思是不变。书的作者认为他所说的这些变化的规律是不可改变的。书中有一些文字，叫做"卦辞"和"爻（yáo）辞"，是用来说明这些符号的。后来又有人写了十篇文章，对《易经》进行解释，叫做《易传》。《易经》是用来算卦的书，《易传》基本上是讲哲学和伦理的。两部书合起来叫做《周易》。

一、"一阴一阳之谓道"。《周易》认为事物都在不断地运动变化，变化的总规律是阴阳两种对立的力量往返交替。比如，太阳落了，月亮会升起来；月亮落了，太阳会升起来；太阳和月亮交替出现就有了光明。冷天过去了，热天就来了；热天过去了，冷天又来了；冷天和热天往返交替就有了岁月。任何事物都是一阴一阳的往返交替，没有一阴一阳的交替就没有运动变化，没有运动变化就没有了生命。事物的存在需要有阴阳两个方面，事物的发展变化也需要有阴阳两个方面，在这两个方面中阳的作用更重要，因为它代表着积极主动。但是只有阳也不行，阳需要有阴的配合才能生成万物并使万物发展变化。比如，有天有地才能有万物，有男有女才能有人类。阴阳两种力量相互作用，相互交替，相反相成，这就叫做"一阴一阳谓之道"。

二、"亢龙有悔"。"亢龙"比喻地位极高而又骄傲自满的皇帝，"有悔"就是遭到失败。一个地位极高的人如果骄傲自满，只知进不知退，只知安不知危，那是迟早要失败的。事物都有阴和阳两个方面，在这两个方面中，阳虽然起主要作用，但是阳的力量也不能过于强大，阳的势力过大了，就会破坏事物之间的平衡。一个国家有君和民两个方面，在这两个方面中，君的地位高、权力大，但是，如果他看不起人民，不尊重人民，那就会被人民赶下台。所以我们无论是做事还是做人，都需要把握好尺度，都需要不骄不躁、谦虚谨慎。

三、"自强不息"。《周易》告诉我们，一个物只有不断地发展变化才能存在，一个人只有不断地进步才能生存。要想进步就要不断地提高自己的道德品质，不断地学习新的知识，不断地增强自己的才干；要想进步就要不怕困难，勇往直前。

王金泰　画

中国古代哲学

生词

jīng diǎn 经典	classic	kàng 亢	excessive; extreme
fú hào 符号	symbol	shì lì 势力	power; influence
jī jí 积极	active	pínghéng 平衡	balance
xiāo jí 消极	passive	quán lì 权力	power; authority
suàn guà 算卦	practice divination	chǐ dù 尺度	measure; scale
lún lǐ 伦理	ethics	bù jiāo bú zào 不骄不躁	free from conceit and impetuosity; neither arrogant nor rash
wǎng fǎn 往返	go to and fro		
jiāo tì 交替	alternately; in turn	qiān xū 谦虚	modest
fāngmiàn 方面	aspect	jǐn shèn 谨慎	cautious; prudent
zuò yòng 作用	effect; function	zì qiáng bù xī 自强不息	work hard to improve oneself
zhǔ dòng 主动	initiative		

听写

符号　积极　方面　权力　交替　不骄不躁　谦虚

往返　平衡　主动　*消极　谨慎

比一比

经 { 经典 / 经验 }　　势 { 势力 / 地势 }　　极 { 积极 / 北极 }　　虚 { 谦虚 / 虚伪 }

动 { 主动 / 运动 / 动机 }　　返 { 往返 / 返回 }　　谦 { 谦虚 / 谦让 }　　替 { 交替 / 代替 }

字词运用

积极

上哲学课时，张华总是积极发言。

姐姐爱唱歌，每次表演她都积极参加。

主动

弟弟从不主动练琴，总要妈妈催。

哥哥主动提出要学中文。

近义词

往返——来回　　　　才干——才能——能力

 中国古代哲学

反义词

光明——黑暗　　　积极——消极　　　阴——阳

运动——静止　　　骄傲——谦虚

根据课文回答问题

1. 什么是《易经》、《易传》、《周易》？

2. "易"的三层意思都是什么？

3. 什么是"八卦"？

4. 请解释《周易》中讲的"一阴一阳之谓道"。

5. 请解释《周易》中的"自强不息"。

词语解释

勇往直前——勇敢地一直往前走。

自强不息——努力向上，永远不放松自己。

骄傲自满——满足于自己已有的成绩，自以为了不起，看不起别人。

相配词语连线

遭到　　　才干

破坏　　　尺度

增强　　　平衡

把握　　　失败

Lesson Eight

Thought of *Yi Jing*
(An Optional Lesson)

Yi Jing (*The Book of Changes*) is a book, and is one of the main Confucian classics. The word "*Yi*" has three meanings: the first meaning is transformation and change since the book discusses changes; the second meaning is "simplicity" because it uses only two symbols to indicate different things and changes: One is "——", called "*yang*", symbolizing the power of heaven, sun, brightness, hardness, activity, motion and warmth; one is "— —", called "*yin*", symbolizing the power of earth, moon, darkness, weakness, passivity, motionless and cold. When these two symbols are combined in a trigram, there will result in eight combinations which are known as the "Eight Trigrams (*Ba Gua*)": qian, kun, kan, li, gen, dui, xun, zhen, respectively symbolizing heaven, earth, water, fire, mountain, marsh, wind and thunder. By combining any two of the these trigrams with one another, a total of sixty-four combinations is obtained which are known as the "sixty-four Hexagrams (*Liushisi Gua*)", indicating the different relations and changes among the things. The third of meaning is "invariability". In the author's opinion, all the laws of changes he mentioned remain invariable. In the book, there are some textual comments called "*Gua Ci*" and "*Yao Ci*" which are used to explain the symbols. Later on, ten articles have been written to interpret systematically the implications of *Yi Jing* and thus formed *Yi Zhuan*. The combination of *Jing* and *Zhuan* makes *Zhou Yi*, in which *Yi Jing* is used to tell fortune while *Yi Zhuan* basically talks about philosophy and ethics. The main principles are as follows:

First, "One *Yang* and one *Yin:* this is called the *Tao*": *Zhou Yi* puts forward that all things are moving and changing all the time and the general law of changes is that the two opposite powers *Yin* and *Yang* are changing by turns. For example, the moon will rise after the sun sets; the sun will rise after the moon sets. The alternative appearance of the sun and the moon brings brightness. After the cold weather was over, the hot weather will come; after the hot weather was over, the cold weather will come. The alternative change between hot weather and cold weather forms the seasons. Any thing alternates between *Yin* and *Yang*, without which there will be no changes. Without changes, there will be no life. Thus, *Yin* and *Yang* are the basic requirements for the existence of all things as well as the changes of things. Comparatively speaking, *Yang* plays a more important role because it represents being active and initiative, but it will not do if there is just only *Yang* because only when *Yang* and *Yin* are joined can everything come into being and develop with changes. For instance, everything can come into existence only after heaven and earth are joined, and human beings come into being only after men and women are joined. *Yin* and *Yang* interact with each other, alternate with each other and complement each other, which is called "One *Yang* and one *Yin*: this is called the *Tao*".

Second, "Arrogant dragon will have cause to repent (*Kanglong you hui*)": "*Kanglong*" refers to the conceited emperor who is in a high social status, while "*you hui*" means getting defeated. A person in a high status will be doomed to failure if he is conceited and only knows how to march forward instead of retreating, if he never thinks of danger in times of peace. The reason for this is that everything has two aspects: *Yin* and *Yang*, and the balance between things will be destroyed if *Yang* is too powerful although *Yang* plays a main role. It is true with a nation, which is composed of the king and people, among which the king is in a high status and powerful. However, he will be forced to be out of the position if he looks down upon the people and disrespect the people. Therefore, when we are learning how to be a man or how to do right things, all of us need to be modest and prudent to an appropriate extent, never be arrogant and conceited.

Third, "Making unceasing efforts to improve oneself": *Zhou Yi* tells us that a thing can exist by keeping changing all the time and a person can only survive by making progress constantly. Making progress calls for constant improvement of one's moralities, unceasing obtaining of new knowledge and keeping enhancing one's abilities; making progress needs to march forward even in face of great difficulties.

生字表（简）

1. 腊(là) 儒(rú) 释(shì) 割(gē) 忠(zhōng) 恕(shù) 施(shī) 遵(zūn) 稳(wěn) 秩(zhì)
2. 恻(cè) 谦(qiān) 义(yì) 栽(zāi) 培(péi)
3. 荀(xún) 联(lián) 御(yù) 锋(fēng) 社(shè)
4. 讨(tǎo) 享(xiǎng) 兼(jiān) 效(xiào)
5. 丑(chǒu) 檐(yán)
6. 霜(shuāng) 耍(shuǎ) 扰(rǎo) 脊(jǐ)
7. 卒(zú) 述(shù) 殆(dài) 案(àn) 蜀(shǔ) 撤(chè) 灶(zào) 渡(dù)
8. 符(fú) 卦(guà) 亢(kàng) 权(quán) 躁(zào) 谨(jǐn) 慎(shèn)

共计 45 个生字

生字表（繁）

1. 臘 儒 釋 割 忠 恕 施 遵 穩 秩
   (là rú shì gē zhōng shù shī zūn wěn zhì)

2. 惻 謙 義 栽 培
   (cè qiān yì zāi péi)

3. 荀 聯 禦 鋒 社
   (xún lián yù fēng shè)

4. 討 享 兼 效
   (tǎo xiǎng jiān xiào)

5. 醜 詹
   (chǒu yán)

6. 霜 耍 擾 脊
   (shuāng shuǎ rǎo jǐ)

7. 卒 述 殆 案 蜀 撤 竈 渡
   (zú shù dài àn shǔ chè zào dù)

8. 符 卦 亢 權 躁 謹 慎
   (fú guà kàng quán zào jǐn shèn)

共計 45 個生字

生词表（简）

1. 教育 jiào yù　希腊 xī là　儒家 rú jiā　学派 xué pài　道德 dào dé　高尚 gāo shàng　解释 jiě shì　感情 gǎn qíng
　精神境界 jīng shén jìng jiè　割断 gē duàn　忠恕 zhōng shù　宽容 kuān róng　施 shī　事业 shì yè　克制 kè zhì　约束 yuē shù
　行为 xíng wéi　遵守 zūn shǒu　规范 guī fàn　稳定 wěn dìng　秩序 zhì xù

2. 理论 lǐ lùn　恻隐 cè yǐn　同情 tóng qíng　羞耻 xiū chǐ　谦让 qiān ràng　善恶 shàn è　区别 qū bié　正义 zhèng yì
　顺利 shùn lì　对待 duì dài　栽 zāi　培养 péi yǎng　根本 gēn běn　领导 lǐng dǎo　人民 rén mín　拥护 yōng hù　爱戴 ài dài
　资格 zī gé

3. 荀子 xún zǐ　伪 wěi　具有 jù yǒu　制度 zhì dù　性质 xìng zhì　功能 gōng néng　规律 guī lǜ　目的 mù dì　联系 lián xì
　依靠 yī kào　改造 gǎi zào　御寒 yù hán　锋利 fēng lì　组织 zǔ zhī　社会 shè huì　集体 jí tǐ　发挥 fā huī　企图 qǐ tú

4. 成果 chéng guǒ　讨论 tǎo lùn　饮料 yǐn liào　生存 shēng cún　占有 zhàn yǒu　享受 xiǎng shòu　兼 jiān　争夺 zhēng duó
　互利 hù lì　动机 dòng jī　效果 xiào guǒ　体现 tǐ xiàn　主张 zhǔ zhāng

5. 充分 chōng fèn　围绕 wéi rào　理解 lǐ jiě　法则 fǎ zé　对立面 duì lì miàn　前提 qián tí　丑 chǒu　坚硬 jiān yìng
　柔软 róu ruǎn　屋檐 wū yán　刚强 gāng qiáng　保持 bǎo chí　夺取 duó qǔ　一旦 yí dàn　具体 jù tǐ　外交 wài jiāo
　内务 nèi wù

中国古代哲学

6. 代表(dài biǎo) 地位(dì wèi) 整个(zhěng gè) 一切(yí qiè) 特征(tè zhēng) 存在(cún zài) 功用(gōng yòng) 霜(shuāng)
戏耍(xì shuǎ) 训练(xùn liàn) 截短(jié duǎn) 顺应(shùn yìng) 打扰(dǎ rǎo) 脊背(jǐ bèi) 凭借(píng jiè) 条件(tiáo jiàn)
融入(róng rù)

7. 卒(zú) 论述(lùn shù) 实业(shí yè) 统帅(tǒng shuài) 纪律(jì lǜ) 严明(yán míng) 殆(dài) 作战(zuò zhàn)
方案(fāng àn) 防守(fáng shǒu) 要害(yào hài) 蜀(shǔ) 撤退(chè tuì) 灶(zào) 保存(bǎo cún) 提拔(tí bá)
威望(wēi wàng) 渡(dù) 指挥(zhǐ huī) 奋勇(fèn yǒng)

8. 经典(jīng diǎn) 符号(fú hào) 积极(jī jí) 消极(xiāo jí) 算卦(suàn guà) 伦理(lún lǐ) 往返(wǎng fǎn) 交替(jiāo tì)
方面(fāng miàn) 作用(zuò yòng) 主动(zhǔ dòng) 亢(kàng) 势力(shì lì) 平衡(píng héng) 权力(quán lì) 尺度(chǐ dù)
不骄不躁(bù jiāo bú zào) 谦虚(qiān xū) 谨慎(jǐn shèn) 自强不息(zì qiáng bù xī)

共计 144 个生词

生詞表（繁）

1. 教育(jiào yù) 希臘(xī là) 儒家(rú jiā) 學派(xué pài) 道德(dào dé) 高尚(gāo shàng) 解釋(jiě shì) 感情(gǎn qíng) 精神境界(jīng shén jìng jiè) 割斷(gē duàn) 忠恕(zhōng shù) 寬容(kuān róng) 施(shī) 事業(shì yè) 克制(kè zhì) 約束(yuē shù) 行為(xíng wéi) 遵守(zūn shǒu) 規範(guī fàn) 穩定(wěn dìng) 秩序(zhì xù)

2. 理論(lǐ lùn) 惻隱(cè yǐn) 同情(tóng qíng) 羞恥(xiū chǐ) 謙讓(qiān ràng) 善惡(shàn è) 區別(qū bié) 正義(zhèng yì) 順利(shùn lì) 對待(duì dài) 栽(zāi) 培養(péi yǎng) 根本(gēn běn) 領導(lǐng dǎo) 人民(rén mín) 擁護(yōng hù) 愛戴(ài dài) 資格(zī gé)

3. 荀子(xún zǐ) 偽(wěi) 具有(jù yǒu) 制度(zhì dù) 性質(xìng zhì) 功能(gōng néng) 規律(guī lǜ) 目的(mù dì) 聯繫(lián xì) 依靠(yī kào) 改造(gǎi zào) 禦寒(yù hán) 鋒利(fēng lì) 組織(zǔ zhī) 社會(shè huì) 集體(jí tǐ) 發揮(fā huī) 企圖(qǐ tú)

4. 成果(chéng guǒ) 討論(tǎo lùn) 飲料(yǐn liào) 生存(shēng cún) 佔有(zhàn yǒu) 享受(xiǎng shòu) 兼(jiān) 爭奪(zhēng duó) 互利(hù lì) 動機(dòng jī) 效果(xiào guǒ) 體現(tǐ xiàn) 主張(zhǔ zhāng)

5. 充分(chōng fèn) 圍繞(wéi rào) 理解(lǐ jiě) 法則(fǎ zé) 對立面(duì lì miàn) 前提(qián tí) 醜(chǒu) 堅硬(jiān yìng) 柔軟(róu ruǎn) 屋簷(wū yán) 剛強(gāng qiáng) 保持(bǎo chí) 奪取(duó qǔ) 一旦(yí dàn) 具體(jù tǐ) 外交(wài jiāo) 內務(nèi wù)

中国古代哲学

6. 代表(dài biǎo) 地位(dì wèi) 整個(zhěng gè) 一切(yí qiè) 特徵(tè zhēng) 存在(cún zài) 功用(gōng yòng) 霜(shuāng)
戲耍(xì shuǎ) 訓練(xùn liàn) 截短(jié duǎn) 順應(shùn yìng) 打擾(dǎ rǎo) 脊背(jǐ bèi) 憑借(píng jiè) 條件(tiáo jiàn)
融入(róng rù)

7. 卒(zú) 論述(lùn shù) 實業(shí yè) 統帥(tǒng shuài) 紀律(jì lǜ) 嚴明(yán míng) 殆(dài) 作戰(zuò zhàn)
方案(fāng àn) 防守(fáng shǒu) 要害(yào hài) 蜀(shǔ) 撤退(chè tuì) 灶(zào) 保存(bǎo cún) 提拔(tí bá)
威望(wēi wàng) 渡(dù) 指揮(zhǐ huī) 奮勇(fèn yǒng)

8. 經典(jīng diǎn) 符號(fú hào) 積極(jī jí) 消極(xiāo jí) 算卦(suàn guà) 倫理(lún lǐ) 往返(wǎng fǎn) 交替(jiāo tì)
方面(fāngmiàn) 作用(zuò yòng) 主動(zhǔ dòng) 亢(kàng) 勢力(shì lì) 平衡(píng héng) 權力(quán lì) 尺度(chǐ dù)
不驕不躁(bù jiāo bú zào) 謙虛(qiān xū) 謹慎(jǐn shèn) 自強不息(zì qiáng bù xī)

共計 144 個生詞

第一课

一 写生词

希	腊											
儒	家											
解	释											
割	断											
忠	恕											
施												
遵	守											
稳	定											
秩	序											

二 组词

哲_____ 稳_____ 割_____ 释_____

德_____ 品_____ 诚_____ 精_____

忠_____ 行_____ 秩_____ 遵_____

三 选字组词

品德高(上　尚)　　发(恕　怒)　　行(为　伪)

精神(竟　境)界　　(克　刻)制　　(尊　遵)守

克(己　已)复礼　　解(译　释)　　(割　害)断

四 写出反义词

有害——　　　　　　　　真诚——

五 选择填空(请将词语写在空白处)

1. 孔子是_____时期的人。(春秋　战国)

2. 孔子创立了_____学派。(儒家　道家)

3. 孔子是个伟大的_____、_____。

(哲学家　天文学家　教育家)

六 选词填空(请将词语写在空白处)

成功　感情　影响　真诚　相连

1. 孔子的思想对于中国和世界都有很大的_____。

2. 爱人要_____,而不能虚情假意。

3. 亲朋好友和你最有_____。

4. 宇宙间一切东西都是血肉_____的。

5. 人都希望得到幸福、快乐和事业的_____。

七 造句

遵守_____

八 词语解释

1. 有益——

2. 真诚——

3. 创立——

九 请简单解释孔子的观点

1. "仁"：_____

2. "忠恕之道"：_____
_____

3. "己所不欲，勿施于人"：_____
_____
_____

十 根据课文回答问题

　　1. 孔子认为最根本、最高尚的品质是什么？

　　答：_____

　　_____

　　2. "克己复礼"的"克己"指的是什么？"复礼"指的是什么？

　　答：_____

　　_____

　　_____

十一 写一写你所知道的孔子（300字左右）

_____

_____

_____

_____

_____

_____

十二 熟读课文

第三课

一 写生词

荀	子											

联	系											

御	寒											

锋	利											

社	会											

二 组词

性_____   惯_____   欲_____   律_____

互_____   联_____   营_____   寒_____

社_____   集_____   限_____   挥_____

锋_____   益_____   功_____   靠_____

改_____   织_____   具_____   目_____

三 写出近义词

区别——　　　　　　　　　　打算——

四 写出反义词

伪——　　　　　　　　　　个人——

五 给多音字注汉语拼音

1. 荀子认为人性是恶的（　　）。

2. 自然界的运动变化并没有什么目的（　　）。

六 选择填空（请把词语写在空白处）

1. 自然界的各种事物都是相互_____、相互依靠的。

（联系　关系）

2. 人能认识自然、利用自然、_____自然。

（改变　改造）

3. 人没有_____的爪牙。（山峰　锋利）

4. 人能利用_____的力量战胜其他事物。

（集中　集体）

5. 应该分清什么是自然界的_____和功能。

（品质　性质）

6. 荀子提出"_____"。（性恶论　性善论）

7. 孟子提出"_____"。（性恶论　性善论）

8. "明于天人之分"是_____提出的。（孔子　荀子）

七　造句

目的_____

八　相配词语连线

制定　　　　秩序

破坏　　　　法规

战胜　　　　教育

接受　　　　高尚

品德　　　　敌人

九　请简单解释荀子的"性恶论"

_____
_____
_____
_____

十　请举例说明什么事物是"有限"的，什么事物是"无限"的

_____
_____
_____
_____

十一　写一写你所知道的荀子（300字左右）

_____
_____
_____
_____

十二　熟读课文

第五课

一 写生词

丑											

屋	檐										

二 组词

理_____　　充_____　　绕_____　　丑_____

坚_____　　软_____　　论_____　　强_____

旦_____　　夺_____　　具_____　　其_____

慧_____　　持_____　　任_____　　衰_____

则_____　　体_____　　提_____

9

三 选字组词(画圈)

（理　里）解　　　（刚　钢）强　　　充（份　分）

屋（沿　檐）　　　围（绕　浇）　　　前（题　提）

一（但　旦）　　　（揉　柔）弱

四 写出近义词

规律——　　　　　　不论——

五 写出反义词

柔弱——　　　　　　美——

柔软——　　　　　　正面——

六 选择填空(请把词语写在空白处)

1. 老子的思想_____体现了中国人的_____。

（充分　充满　才智　智慧）

2. 老子的思想是围绕着对"道"的_____展开的。

（理论　理解）

3. 天地万物都有它发展变化的_____。

（规定　规律）

4. 弱小的事物能够_____强大的事物。

（战胜　胜利）

5. 任何事物_____强大了，也就会逐渐衰落了。

（但是　一旦）

6. "无为"就是不去做任何_____的事情。

（具有　具体）

七　选词填空（请把词语写在空白处）

生存　　保持　　刚强　　状态　　无论

"柔弱胜_____"说的是_____一个人还是一个国家，要想长期_____下去，就要_____柔弱的_____。

八　造句

一旦_____

九 解释下列老子的观点

1. "反者道之动"

2. "柔弱胜刚强"

十 举三个例子说明每一种事物都有自己的对立面

十一 写一写你所知道的老子（300字左右）

_____

_____

_____

_____

_____

十二 熟读课文

第七课

一 写生词

卒												

论	述											

殉												

方	案											

蜀												

撤	退											

灶												

渡												

二 组词

述_____ 存_____ 实_____ 帅_____

威_____ 渡_____ 勇_____ 防_____

训_____ 提_____ 拔_____ 撤_____

纪_____ 统_____ 要_____ 指_____

三 选字组词

包(括 舌)　　（做 作）战　　作(业 叶)

统(师 帅)　　（方 防）案　　提(拔 拨)

撤(退 腿)　　（纪 记）律　　情(况 兄)

四 写出近义词

卒——　　　　　　　打仗——

五 选择填空（请把词语写在空白处）

1. 孙子是中国古代伟大的_____家。（哲学　军事）

2. 《孙子兵法》_____地论述了战争中的各种问题。

（系统　传统）

3. 军队的纪律必须_____。（严厉　严明）

4. 作战要_____敌我双方的情况。（懂得　了解）

5. 战争中要进攻敌人的_____。（要害　厉害）

6. 战争中双方都会努力_____敌人，_____自己。

（消失　消灭　保存　保持）

六 选词填空（请把词语写在空白处）

威望　　生存　　带领　　不利

1. 赵国城市的地形对韩信的军队非常_____。

2. 韩信是新提拔的将领，_____不高。

3. 韩信_____军队坐船渡过大河后就把船烧掉了。

4. 我们无路可逃，只有打败敌人，我们才能_____。

七 造句

1. 了解_____

2. 保存_____

八 相配词语连线

打败　　　　　　情况

了解　　　　　　军队

制定　　　　　　敌人

指挥　　　　　　方案

九 根据课文回答问题

《孙子兵法》一书是谁写的,在什么时代写的?
答:_____
_____

十 请解释孙子"知己知彼,百战不殆"的观点

_____
_____

十一 熟读课文

第一课听写

第三课听写

第五课听写

第七课听写

练习纸

第二课

一 写生词

恻	隐											
谦	让											
正	义											
栽												
培	养											

二 组词

端_____   善_____   拥_____   仁_____

栽_____   顺_____   谦_____   基_____

羞_____   护_____   逐_____   培_____

管_____   拥_____   义_____   待_____

理_____   顺_____   爱_____   资_____

三 选字组词

（尊 遵）守　　（栽 载）种　　（继 记）承

（尊 遵）敬　　记（栽 载）　　（记 继）录

（事 是）非　　道（得 德）　　（歉 谦）让

（事 是）情　　获（得 德）　　道（歉 谦）

四 读一读，比一比

端着——端正　　　　害羞——羞耻

礼貌——面貌　　　　亚军——亚圣

区别——地区　　　　发展——头发

正义——意思　　　　间断——时间

五 填空

1. 孟子是孔子的主要_____人之一，被中国人尊称为_____。

2. 对于人为什么会有道德的问题，孟子提出了_____的理论。

六 选词填空(请把词语写在空白处)

礼　　仁　　智　　义

1. 孟子认为"恻隐之心"会发展成为_____,"羞恶之心"会发展成为_____,"辞让之心"会发展成为_____,"是非之心"会发展成为_____。

拔苗助长　　逐渐　　不间断

2. 孟子认为人的道德品质是_____培养起来的,既要_____地努力,又不要_____。

七 造句

1. 爱护_____
2. 说明_____
3. 逐渐_____

八 词语解释

1. 是非——
2. 急于求成——

九　请写一写"拔苗助长"的故事（至少写四句话）

_____

_____

_____

_____

十　请写一写孟子"仁政"的思想（至少写五句话）

_____

_____

_____

_____

_____

十一　熟读课文

第四课

一 写生词

讨	论											

享	受											

兼												

效	果											

二 组词

讨_____   蹄_____   获_____   饮_____

动_____   占_____   享_____   受_____

兼_____   交_____   效_____   欺_____

张_____   夺_____   壮_____   实_____

存_____   利_____   成_____   德_____

三 选字组词

主（张　章）　　（站　占）立　　（效　校）果

文（张　章）　　（站　占）有　　学（效　校）

（争　挣）夺　　（培　倍）养　　讨（论　轮）

（争　挣）扎　　几（培　倍）　　（论　轮）流

四 选择填空（请把词语写在空白处）

1. 人必须通过劳动才能有衣穿、有饭吃，才能_____。

（存在　生存）

2. 不劳动而占有别人的劳动_____是不道德的。

（结果　成果）

3. 以大欺小，以强欺弱，以富欺贫都是不_____的。

（道德　品质）

4. 如果人与人、国与国之间都能互相爱，世界上就没有_____，没有战争了。　　（夺取　争夺）

五 选词填空（请把词语写在空白处）

重视　　手工业者　　重要　　讨论　　创立

墨子是中国_____的思想家、哲学家。他_____了墨家学派。墨子和他的学生大多数是_____，他们都很_____劳动和劳动成果，经常_____劳动的问题。

六 词语解释

不劳而获——

七 根据课文回答问题

1. 墨子创立的学派叫什么？

答：_____

2. 墨子提出的"兼相爱"与孔子讲的"爱人"有什么不同？

答：_____

_____

3. 墨子提出:"每一个人都应该劳动,人只有参加劳动才能享受劳动成果,不劳而获是不道德的。"你的看法是什么?

答:＿＿＿＿＿＿＿＿＿＿＿＿＿＿＿＿＿＿＿＿＿＿＿

＿＿＿＿＿＿＿＿＿＿＿＿＿＿＿＿＿＿＿＿＿＿＿＿＿

＿＿＿＿＿＿＿＿＿＿＿＿＿＿＿＿＿＿＿＿＿＿＿＿＿

八 熟读课文

第六课

一 写生词

霜	雪											

戏	耍											

打	扰											

脊	背											

二 组词

融_____ 括_____ 忘_____ 随_____

庄_____ 代_____ 表_____ 征_____

整_____ 条_____ 训_____ 脊_____

需_____ 耍_____ 凭_____ 遮_____

扰_____ 切_____ 任_____ 存_____

三 选字组词

（代 带）表　　（功 工）能　　戏（要 耍）

（代 带）领　　（功 工）作　　（要 耍）求

必（需 须）　　恐（惧 具）　　打（绕 扰）

（需 须）要　　（惧 具）有　　围（绕 扰）

四 写出近义词

一切——　　　　　　　依靠——

五 写出反义词

无限——

六 选择填空（请将词语写在空白处）

1. 庄子是_____学派的。（儒家　道家）

2. 自然而然，顺应自然，是_____的观点。

（儒家　道家）

3. 庄子的思想也是_____着"道"展开的。

（环绕　围绕）

4. 如果把鹤的腿_____短了，它就不能生活了。

（截　栽）

七　造句

1. 一切_____

2. 代表_____

八　相配词语连线

整个　　　　　　地位

打败　　　　　　事物

很高的　　　　　宇宙

一切　　　　　　敌人

九 根据课文回答问题

庄子认为："人应该尊重自然、顺应自然，而不要按照自己的愿望去改变自然、破坏自然、打扰自然。只有这样，世界才能更好地存在，人类才能更好地生存。"

你是怎样理解庄子的观点的？

答：_____

_____

_____

_____

十 熟读课文

第八课

一 写生词

符	号											
算	卦											
亢												
权	力											
谨	慎											
不	骄	不	躁									

二 组词

伦_____   喻_____   断_____   度_____

列_____   寒_____   明_____   暗_____

典_____   符_____   积_____   消_____

替_____   静_____   卦_____   返_____

自强_____   不骄_____   勇往_____

三 选字组词

经（点　典）　　简（明　名）　　排（例　列）
顶（点　典）　　著（明　名）　　举（例　列）

往（反　返）　　急（燥　躁）　　（歉　谦）虚
正（反　返）　　干（燥　躁）　　道（歉　谦）

自（满　瞒）
隐（满　瞒）

四 读一读

骄傲自满　　谦虚谨慎　　勇往直前　　不骄不躁
积极主动　　往返交替　　相反相成　　自强不息

五 写出近义词

来回——　　　　　　　　　　才干——

六 写出反义词

光明——　　　　　骄傲——　　　　　阴——

消极——　　　　　运动——

七 选词填空

《易传》　　《周易》　　《易经》

1. _____是儒家经典之一,是用来算卦的书。_____基本上是讲哲学和伦理的,是对《易经》的解释。《易经》和《易传》两部书合起来叫做_____。

事物的变化　　规律不变　　简明

2. "易"有三层意思,第一层是讲_____,第二层意思是_____,第三层是讲_____。

━━━　　━ ━

3. 阴的符号是_____;阳的符号是_____。

八 造句

积极_____

九 词语解释

1. 勇往直前——
2. 自强不息——
3. 骄傲自满——

十 根据课文回答问题

1. 什么是"一阴一阳之谓道"?

答:_____
_____
_____

2. 如何理解《周易》中讲的"自强不息"的观点?

答:_____
_____
_____
_____

十一 熟读课文

第二课听写

第四课听写

第六课听写

中国古代哲学

第八课听写

练习纸

中国古代哲学

练习纸

中国古代哲学